P9-BYB-077

What You Need To Know About...

JEHOVAH'S WITNESSES

LORRI MACGREGOR

HARVEST HOUSE PUBLISHERS
EUGENE, OREGON 97402

**WHAT YOU NEED TO KNOW ABOUT
JEHOVAH'S WITNESSES**

Copyright © 1992 by Harvest House Publishers
Eugene, Oregon 97402

Library of Congress Cataloging-in-Publication Data

MacGregor, Lorri, 1942– .
    What you need to know about Jehovah's Witnesses / Lorri
MacGregor.
    ISBN 0-89081-944-0
    1. Jehovah's Witnesses.   I. Title.
    BX8526.5.M33   1992   91-37857
    289.9'2—dc20   CIP

Printed in the United States of America.

CONTENTS

Introduction

INTRODUCTION

The success of the video *The Witness at Your Door* prompted many requests for additional written materials on the subject of presenting Jesus to the Jehovah's Witnesses.

Initially MacGregor Ministries, in cooperation with Jeremiah Films, produced a written insert for each video, outlining the Scriptures used in the video.

Due to the demand for this printed material, MacGregor Ministries next published a booklet of the same name.

It became evident that many churches wanted more. Many became motivated to teach a Sunday school or Bible study course aimed at equipping their members to witness effectively to Jehovah's Witnesses.

At this point Jeremiah Films was marketing a "Pastor's Package" on some of their videos. This package included the video, a book of the same name, a teacher's manual, and Questions for Students, as well as an audiotape of the subject covered. This equipped the churches to teach a course using all these prepared aids. We found the concept exciting and agreed to expand our video *The Witness at Your Door* into this format.

The end product has exceeded even our expectations for it. This book greatly expands on the information in the video, giving Christian readers the information they need to effectively present Jesus to Jehovah's Witnesses. Because the book follows the story line of the video, the reading is not heavy, but more like a novel.

The Bible translation used throughout is the New American Standard Bible. This translation was chosen because of the clarity of the translation, as well as the reluctance of Jehovah's Witnesses to accept the Authorized King James Version. Unfortunately, Jehovah's Witnesses have a programmed prejudice against the King James Version and are taught to mistrust it. Therefore it is not as effective as newer versions when dealing with Jehovah's Witnesses.

The author, once a Jehovah's Witness herself, understands firsthand how Jehovah's Witnesses think and reason. Therefore these presentations on Jesus Christ actually work, having proven themselves over the last 16 years of ministry to Jehovah's Witnesses. May God bless you as you reach out to them and set them free!

CHAPTER 1

♦

Candidates for Cults

Vulnerable. Hurting. Disillusioned. Disappointed. Seeking. Searching. Hungry for spiritual fulfillment. Lonely. Depressed. Stressed-out.

All these words describe a candidate for cult involvement. Christians saved by grace could have periods in their life when they are vulnerable, which explains why cults draw many of their followers out of the Christian church.

Even more at risk are those persons who have not had a spiritual side to their lives, but at some point begin seeking for God. Such a person was Joe Simpson.

Joe should have been satisfied with his life. After all, he had a wife, Brenda, whom he loved. She had been his high school sweetheart. He had a daughter, Lisa, whom he adored. He got a job at the local manufacturing plant after graduating from high school, and things proceeded along relatively smoothly for about ten years. During this time Joe and Brenda bought a modest house in the suburbs, paid their bills, participated in the community, and never worried much about the future.

The closing of the plant was a shock. Joe found

himself competing with many others for too-few jobs. He had no training in other fields. After fruit-less job searches lasting many months, Joe felt defeated and humiliated. Increasingly he took his unemployment checks and spent his time with his buddies in the bar. One night, after an all-day bout of drinking, he went home with a woman he met in the bar and spent the night with her.

He woke up with a hangover, feeling guilty and ashamed. He went home to Brenda. She was fed up with him and took his daughter and left, with every intention of divorcing him for his adultery. They had an angry and tearful parting.

Two hurting and lost souls (not to forget the third victim, their daughter Lisa), now became candidates for the cults. Where once they were secure in their family, now they were broken. Where once they thought they had all the answers, now they had none. Unfortunately, no one in their immediate family had any answers for them either. Everyone suffered.

Both Joe and Brenda ended up crying out to God for help. Brenda did some of her crying in a Chris-tian church and found Christ. Joe did his crying alone in his home, where he was accessible to the cults knocking at his door. Both Brenda and Joe were vulnerable. One ended up with the real Jesus Christ in her life, while the other ended up with a counterfeit Jesus in his life, controlling him through a harsh elder system in a strict cult.

How did an ordinary person like Joe find himself in these circumstances? It started with the doorbell ringing, apparently in answer to his cry for help from God.

CHAPTER 2

◆

Trapping the Honest-Hearted

The beginning seemed harmless enough. A bleary-eyed, unshaven Joe answered the door. He had been without Brenda and Lisa for some days now, and was very lonely and despondent.

He was less than thrilled to see two Jehovah's Witnesses at his door, but they were friendly to him and were not asking for any money. They only wanted his time. Well, he had plenty of time, being unemployed, and they would be a diversion at least. He did not know how vulnerable he was. After all, how much harm could there be in a "Bible study"? Didn't his late grandmother study her Bible? Nothing else had worked in his life, so maybe God would. He got his grandmother's Bible, ready to begin a study of a totally unfamiliar book. He wiped the dust off and prepared to study with an open mind.

The elders quickly disposed of this family Bible, presenting him with their "modern English translation" so his studying would be "easier." They ridiculed the "Old English" found in his Bible. Joe agreed that he would probably understand a modern translation better, so grandmother's Bible went back on the shelf. After all, the Jehovah's Witnesses seemed so sincere and friendly and really seemed to care about him. The indoctrination began.

What Joe did not realize was that his mind was truly being programmed. The Bible was not being studied as it was written. Rather, Joe was referred to isolated and often out-of-context verses to "prove" statements being made in Watch Tower literature.

He was given a publication of the Watch Tower Society. Each one took turns reading a paragraph, and then Joe answered the question at the bottom of the page from the paragraph just read. Every time he gave the correct response he was warmly praised and felt good about himself. The elders patiently showed him how to find Bible verses, and encouraged him to read one now and again to "prove" the point they had just made.

Joe didn't realize that "Bible" study could be so easy and interesting. He was taught to be thankful for God's organization, which provided such easy-to-understand publications. As the weeks passed, he soon found the books of the Bible almost as quickly as the elders, and proudly read his isolated Scriptures. Now he studied ahead of time and prepared for their weekly visits. He answered the questions before the paragraph was read.

Oh, he questioned a few things they taught in the beginning, but his misgivings were quickly "corrected" with Scriptures. He was no match for the well-trained elders. He was swept along with the tide. He was convicted of the truth of what they taught. He even learned to call the teachings he received "the truth." He learned to mistrust the churches, or "Christendom," as the elders called them all. He even mimicked the slight sneer used every time Christian churches or their doctrines were mentioned. How blind they were, in contrast to the "light" he was receiving from "Jehovah's organization"! Ah, yes, the churches didn't even know or use God's name, "Jehovah." How privileged he was to be one of the "sheep"!

Yes, Joe was developing a whole new vocabulary. Each cult has its own terminology that isolates it from the mainstream. Joe could now use terms like "theocracy," "organization," "good news of the kingdom," "great crowd," "remnant," "144,000," "faithful and discreet slave," etc. and be part of the chosen few who understood such terms. Some were Bible terms, but had been given special false definitions by the cult group.

Joe was eventually introduced to the counterfeit Christ of the Jehovah's Witnesses. By the presentation of carefully selected, isolated Scriptures, he was taught that Jesus Christ was the Archangel Michael in heaven while also being "a god." While on earth, he was told, Jesus was only a good man who was always inferior to Jehovah God.

Joe came to believe that after Jesus' death, Jehovah God "recreated" Him as the Archangel Michael in the heavens once more, and that He now directed Jehovah's organization through His angels. The exclusive use of the New World Translation of the Jehovah's Witnesses made all these distortions possible. Joe never thought to check out what he was learning with grandma's Bible.

He did not know that the Bible from the Jehovah's Witnesses had removed or distorted the references to the deity of Jesus Christ. He thought he was being taught the Word of God.

Eventually the Jehovah's Witnesses became Joe's only friends. Where Joe's own efforts to find employment failed, he soon found a job with a local "brother." Now he heard "the truth" all day long at his workplace. Joe was impressed with the honesty and integrity of the "brothers" he worked with. He was totally under the influence of the Jehovah's Witnesses. What he didn't know was that they were doing all these things for him for a reason!

All the Jehovah's Witnesses spending time discussing the Society's doctrines with him were earning their own salvation. They were carefully keeping track of all the minutes they spent with him and reporting this as "field service" at the Kingdom Hall. (Jehovah's Witnesses just love counting time with willing listeners. It cuts down on the time they must spend in the more difficult door-to-door work.) Also, it was high time that Joe became a productive member of their group. All cooperated to bring this about.

Joe was encouraged to enroll in the "Theocratic Ministry School" to learn how to "preach the good news of the kingdom." He sat in on the "Service Meetings," which are the equivalent of motivational meetings held by direct-sales organizations. Quotas are stressed, methods of placing literature are taught, and everyone is made to feel that he or she must do more for Jehovah.

By now Joe was fully integrated into the tight little world of Jehovah's Witnesses. On Sundays he attended the "public talk," a one-hour lecture on various topics. Afterward he participated in a study of the assigned *Watchtower* article. It was similar to his home study in that questions based on the paragraph in the *Watchtower* were answered and then the paragraph read.

The person conducting the study made sure that all the points brought out by the Society were covered. No personal comments or questions were tolerated. No one dared question doctrine. Joe found out just how meek a "sheep" must be to function in Jehovah's Organization under the "shepherds" or "elders." He was proud to be obedient, and was praised for his meekness.

On an assigned day of the week Joe went to an assigned location for the weekly "Book Study." This again was a repeat of the now-familiar method of learning. Fellowship afterward was discouraged. Sometimes someone would go out with him for coffee at a local restaurant, but most times he returned home to an empty house. How preferable it was to be in the company of "brothers and sisters"! Joe was glad he had five meetings a week to attend; it made his loneliness easier to bear.

Brenda had been in contact with him a few times, and he had seen Lisa on occasion, but they drew away from him when he tried to share his new beliefs. Brenda was threatening to leave the area and take Lisa with her.

Joe often shared his concerns about his family with his friend, Elder Leo Stern, who had become a father figure to him. Due to Brenda's coolness to the overtures made by Joe on behalf of the Jehovah's Witnesses, Elder Stern was not hopeful that there could be a reconciliation between Joe and Brenda. Brenda's unwillingness to forgive Joe freed him to divorce her, Joe was repeatedly told.

Soon Joe noticed that he was being encouraged by several divorced and remarried couples in the congregation to do the same. Namely, he should let the unbeliever "depart" (Scriptures were quoted from 1 Corinthians 7), and he should remarry a strong Jehovah's Witness woman. Joe could not help but notice that women were in the majority at the Kingdom Hall, and many of them were single, for various reasons. Some were aggressively looking for husbands in the organization. He knew he was a target.

However, Joe felt that his marriage breakup was his fault, even though he was assured that his act of adultery dissolved his old marriage. He was told he would not be held accountable, since it happened before he knew Jehovah. All he needed to do, he was told by the elders, was make it legal with a divorce decree, freeing him to remarry within the organization.

An attractive divorcée was paying lots of attention to him at the meetings, sitting down beside him and letting him know that his interest in her would be returned. She had a son who needed a father.

Every time someone had him over, there she was! Joe felt the pressure to conform to what the elders wanted, but in his heart he still loved his wife and daughter. Fortunately for Joe, this one hesitation on this one point prevented his total and absolute commitment to the Jehovah's Witnesses. In every other way, however, he was completely controlled by them.

CHAPTER 3

◆

Committing the Candidate to the Cult

A great deal of time and energy is spent on new recruits coming into cult groups, but there comes a time when the recruit must commit to the group and take his place as a productive member. The recruit is always required to make some kind of public show of his newfound dedication to the group.

In the case of Jehovah's Witnesses, a public baptism at one of their conventions marks the recruit's decision to be one of them. It is no easy matter to be baptized as one of Jehovah's Witnesses. The recruit must have previously shown his willingness to study, attend meetings, train for the field service, and actually go house to house before baptism is considered.

Once a recruit bows to the pressure to be baptized as a Jehovah's Witness, he must embark on further study of the subject. Once prepared, he must submit to a long list of questions regarding his loyalty to the organization and its doctrines. Only upon completion of this grilling is he issued a certificate indicating that he is a candidate for baptism. He is then registered at the convention as a baptismal candidate and undergoes the actual baptism by immersion in water.

The *Watchtower* magazine of June 1, 1985, page 30, says of baptism:

> Before reaching this point of baptism, all candidates have carefully reviewed with congregation elders the Bible's principal doctrines and guidelines for Christian conduct to make sure they really qualify for baptism. Thus the decision to be baptized is by no means a sudden emotional reaction. Rather, each one has "proved for himself the good and acceptable and perfect will of God" and wishes to submit to that will (Romans 12:2).

Of course, prior to baptism the elders make sure the candidate understands that "the good and acceptable and perfect will of God" is nothing less than absolute obedience to the Watch Tower Organization.

In fact, after all this, and just prior to the actual baptism, each candidate answers two questions. The first question is:

> On the basis of the sacrifice of Jesus Christ, have you repented of your sins and dedicated yourself to Jehovah to do his will?

The candidate answers yes, understanding this to mean that he is dedicated to Jehovah God through the Watch Tower Organization.

The second question which the baptismal candidate must answer is very revealing:

> Do you understand that your dedication and baptism identify you as one of Jehovah's Witnesses in association with God's Spirit-directed organization?

The *Watchtower* article from which these questions are taken (June 1, 1985, page 30) then goes on to state:

> Having answered yes to these questions, candidates are in a right heart condition to undergo Christian baptism.

What a long, drawn-out ordeal to be baptized as one of Jehovah's Witnesses! Rather than being baptized because of repentance of sins and belief in the Lord Jesus Christ, as were all examples in the Bible, Jehovah's Witnesses must be baptized in the name of the organization and thereafter submit to it.

Consider these Bible examples of baptism, and how different they are from the baptismal instructions of the Jehovah's Witnesses. The eunuch was preached to by Philip as they traveled along together in a chariot. Acts 8:36-38 records:

> As they went along the road they came to some water; and the eunuch said, "Look! Water! What prevents me from being baptized?" [And Philip said, "If you believe with all your heart, you may." And he

> answered and said, "I believe that Jesus
> Christ is the Son of God."] And he ordered
> the chariot to stop; and they both went
> down into the water, Philip as well as the
> eunuch; and he baptized him.

The account goes on to record that the "Spirit of
the Lord" was present at the baptism. No long,
drawn-out preparations here, nor any declaration
of dedication to an organization—just belief in the
Lord Jesus Christ. All this apparently happened
within the space of a few hours. How different from
the months or even years of painstaking preparation required by the Jehovah's Witnesses!

Likewise, Lydia heard the gospel and was baptized the same day as she "opened her heart" (see
Acts 16:14,15).

The jailer and his household believed in the Lord
Jesus Christ, and verse 33 of Acts chapter 16 records
that their baptism occurred *immediately*:

> ... and immediately he was baptized, he
> and all his household.

Yes, the Bible examples of baptism bear no resemblance to the tedious process of the Jehovah's Witnesses. Baptism is a joyous occasion in a believer's
life and emotions are involved (contrary to Watch
Tower teachings), especially the good emotion of
the committing of one's heart to the Lord Jesus
Christ and the inviting of Him to be Lord of one's
life.

Another important step in a recruit's commitment to the Jehovah's Witness organization is to

engage in the "house-to-house" preaching work. Actually, this is nothing more than placing the Society's literature in people's homes and conducting "Bible" studies. These are really studies of the Society's strange interpretations of Scriptures out of their own publications. This part of the Society's activities is run like a direct sales organization, with similar methods of motivation. The Society collects money for their literature "up front" at the Kingdom Hall, from their own people, by direct charge or donation. Now Jehovah's Witnesses are expected to request donations at the doors as well and turn this money in at the Kingdom Halls. This recent practice is increasing the wealth of the Watch Tower Society dramatically.

Jehovah's Witnesses are motivated into the difficult door-to-door activity (which most of them dislike) by the misuse of isolated Scriptures. For example, Matthew 10:12-14 might be used to get them going:

> As you enter the house, give it your greeting. And if the house is worthy, let your greeting of peace come upon it; but if it is not worthy, let your greeting of peace return to you. And whoever does not receive you, nor heed your words, as you go out of that house or that city, shake off the dust of your feet.

This misused Scripture is necessary for the Jehovah's Witness training, since most calls will be unreceptive, but the Jehovah's Witness must still be made to feel that he is doing God's will. Many self-righteously feel that their work decides the householder's fate on judgment day and go away quite smugly from unreceptive doors.

However, is this Scripture talking about the present-day work of Jehovah's Witnesses, or even anything similar to it? Not at all. As in all Scriptures, we must consider the context or setting. If we look at the previous verse we find the context:

> Into whatever city or village you enter, inquire who is worthy in it; and abide there until you go away (Matthew 10:11).

Notice that the disciples were traveling and therefore entering cities or villages. Notice also that they were to "abide" at that one house to which they gave a greeting in verse 12. Obviously these Scriptures referred to the subject of *accommodation* for the disciples. Calling at every house was not even implied in this account!

Furthermore, if we read the entire chapter of Matthew 10 we find out other interesting facts, such as to whom the disciples were sent and what they actually did.

Verse 6 makes it plain that they were sent to the *Jews only*, not Gentiles at this time, and that their message was "The Kingdom of heaven is at hand" (verse 7). Notice their activities in verse 8:

> Heal the sick, raise the dead, cleanse the lepers, cast out demons; freely you received, freely give.

Could we even remotely apply these Scriptures to Jehovah's Witnesses? Never! They do not believe in heaven except for 144,000 of their select members, so they are not preaching the "kingdom of heaven" at the door. Rather, they stress their peculiar doctrine of living on earth, which is arrived at by out-of-context Scriptures as well.

Secondly, they do not do the same work as the disciples at all. The dynamic ministry of the disciples bears no resemblance to the dreary and boring presentations of the Jehovah's Witnesses at the doors, trying to pass off the Society's publications as truth! You may wish to read parallel accounts about the ministry in Jesus' day in Mark 6 and Luke 9.

Despite the claims of Jehovah's Witnesses to be "footstep followers" of Jesus, we can find no resemblance between their ministry and that of Jesus Christ and his early disciples.

Some of the other times when Jesus and His disciples were spoken of as being in houses, they were obviously guests, not door-to-door drop-ins. Other times they were visiting the churches that met in the various houses. In fact, the Bible phrase "house to house" means "church to church," since believers were gathered in houses. Disciples traveled from "house to house" (or church to church) for the purpose of teaching and encouraging the believers.

Let's consider some Scriptures showing that the early church met in houses.

In Paul's greeting to Prisca and Aquila, he continues in Romans 16:5:

Greet the church that is in their house (see also 1 Corinthians 16:19).

Again, we read in Colossians 4:15:

Greet the brethren who are in Laodicea and also Nympha and the church that is in her house.

Again, in Philemon 1:2:

... to Apphia our sister, and to Archippus our fellow soldier, and to the church in your house.

These Scriptures show that the apostles ministered to the believers gathered in various houses having meetings. The apostles went "house to house."

Finally, we will consider the all-time favorite "proof text" of Jehovah's Witnesses for going house to house. Acts 20:20 reads:

... how I did not shrink from declaring to you anything that was profitable, and teaching you publicly and from house to house (NWT).

Now let's examine the true context: "... declaring to you..." Who is this "you"? Verses 17 and 18 of Acts 20 tells us to whom Paul was speaking:

From Miletus he sent to Ephesus and called to him the elders of the church. And when they had come to him, he said to them. ...

Yes, Paul was speaking to the elders of the church, not to random people he contacted house to house! Instructions to the church make up the rest of Paul's discourse.

Once again, Jehovah's Witnesses have no biblical basis for their house-to-house work. There is no biblical command against going house to house, but neither is there a Bible precedent, and Jehovah's Witnesses should not attempt to invent one.

Jesus and His disciples did preach in the Jewish temples, and they did speak to crowds out of doors, but they did *not* organize themselves and call house to house on everybody. Rather, people sought them out because of the evident working of God in their lives, and the witness of others. If modern-day Jehovah's Witnesses did not call door-to-door, who would ever seek them out?

Although Luke 10:7 refers to the disciples seeking accommodation, since Jehovah's Witnesses use such Scriptures inaccurately to further their house-to-house work, I suggest that they use this one also:

Do not keep moving from house to house.

Poor Joe Simpson! Here he was baptized and committed, calling house to house, trying to work out his own salvation in obedience to an organization. No one within that organization could or would show him the real truth.

Joe's only hope now was that behind one of the doors on which he knocked would be a true Christian equipped to witness the true gospel to him— one who would patiently help to set him free from bondage, with the help of the Lord. Would he ever encounter one, or would he be like thousands of other Jehovah's Witnesses calling at homes year after year, never finding a Christian willing to help?

CHAPTER 4

Preparing for Ministry to Jehovah's Witnesses

Beverly Williams was a dedicated Christian. She lived her faith in word and deed. Her heart would regularly ache for the lost. Growing up in the church, she had been stirred by the missionary reports she heard. She had intended to be a missionary one day, but life got in the way. She ended up being a Christian wife and mother, active in her own church, and helping others where she could.

One day while watching the Jehovah's Witnesses going about in her neighborhood she felt the familiar ache for the lost. As she bowed her head and said a prayer for their salvation, she was struck by the thought that she could be a missionary to them! Here was a mission field coming right up to her own door! She excitedly called her pastor about her new idea, but to her surprise he was less than enthusiastic. He read to her 2 John 10,11 in a solemn voice:

> If anyone comes to you and does not bring this teaching, do not receive him into your house, and do not give him a greeting; for the one who gives him a greeting participates in his evil deeds.

Not only was she discouraged about her "missions call," but now she was told she must not even greet these lost ones or invite them in! She went immediately to prayer to God for guidance and began to read the second epistle of John over and over, believing that God would help her with her dilemma.

During this time she saw an ex-Jehovah's Witness on television, telling of her deliverance from that cult and giving a glowing testimony for Christ. She had been witnessed to by a Christian, and with other willing workers she now taught Christians how to reach Jehovah's Witnesses with the gospel.

Beverly Williams was curious enough to write to the ministry outreach operated by this person, and read with interest a tract sent back to her. She read:

Should You Dialogue with
Jehovah's Witnesses?

Some Christians use 2 John 10,11 to be rude and unresponsive to Jehovah's Witnesses. It reads:

> If anyone comes to you and does not bring this teaching, do not receive him into your house, and do not give him a greeting; for the one who gives him a greeting participates in his evil deeds.

However, this Scripture in context is not referring to the unsaved Jehovah's Witness at your door who has been deceived by the Watch Tower Society.

To understand the context we must look to the previous verses. Notice in verses 1 and 2 of 2 John that this epistle was written to believers:

The elder to the chosen lady and her children, whom I love in truth, and not only I, but also all who know the truth, for the sake of the truth which abides in us and will be with us forever.

Verse 7 begins:

For many deceivers have gone out into the world.

Gone out from where? Obviously from the congregation of believers to whom this letter was written. Verse 9 identifies them further as—

anyone who goes too far and does not abide in the teaching of Christ.

This description could well apply to the early leadership of Jehovah's Witnesses who left the historic Christian church, adopted the Arian heresy, and did not abide in the biblical teaching of Christ. Their followers, however, usually the ones at your door, do not fit into this category of "deceivers." They are not deliberately misrepresenting Christ, but are thoroughly deceived by their leaders. They never abode in the true doctrine of Christ and then left, because they never knew it in the first place. Therefore 2 John does not apply to them.

The Jesus of the Jehovah's Witnesses

Jehovah's Witnesses deny the trinity and deny that Jesus is or ever was Almighty God. Instead, they reduce Him to the Archangel Michael in the heavens, only a good man on earth, and again Michael in the heavens after his resurrection. They admit that Jesus is "a god," but not "the God."

Remember, we as Christians are to bear witness for Christ. We do not have to do the work of the Holy Spirit, that of convicting people of their sin. God will look after that if we are faithful to let Him. I believe our instructions on witnessing are summed up very nicely in 2 Timothy 2:24-26:

> The Lord's bondservant must not be quarrelsome, but be kind to all, able to teach, patient when wronged, with gentleness correcting those who are in opposition, if perhaps God may grant them repentance leading to the knowledge of the truth, and they may come to their senses and escape from the snare of the devil, having been held captive by him to do his will.

Remember to Pray

Do not attempt to pray with the Jehovah's Witness, but pray ahead of time for the next ones who will come. If they surprise you, excuse yourself for a few moments and then pray before you speak with them. Remember, you must fight spiritual battles with spiritual weapons. Take your authority in Jesus' name and bind the spirit of deception operating in their lives, asking God to help you say the right things to set them free. Then prepare yourself with several appropriate scriptural points.

Beverly Williams was convicted in her own heart to begin her missions work, but first she knew she must prepare in the same way that any missionary prepares for the mission field.

Namely, she must learn the beliefs, background, and customs of the people she was about to minister to, so that she would be effective. However, since the best teacher is experience, she decided to begin immediately by learning a simple presentation suggested by this ministry to the cults, which allowed her to share just one Scripture and then present her testimony.

She recognized that she could not spend all her time studying obscure doctrines, but must focus her preparation on the most important topic, the Lord Jesus Christ. She was determined to deal with the errors of the Jehovah's Witnesses concerning Jesus point by point, beginning with the error that He was Michael the Archangel, and then moving on to the deeper teachings concerning His deity.

She recognized that she must fight spiritual battles with spiritual weapons, and so she made prayer her chief weapon, relying on the Holy Spirit to help her. She thanked God for the specialized ministries to the cults who prepared so much good information she could learn quickly.

It took a much shorter time than she thought to prepare herself to start winning souls and to defend the gospel of Christ to Jehovah's Witnesses. There was such an abundance of material available on the topic. She knew that if she got stuck she could always contact the cults ministries to help her along.

However, if she controlled the encounters and discussed the topics she knew, she should now do quite well, with the Lord's help. She reasoned that even if she failed, at least she had tried her best, and that was preferable to saying nothing to the lost.

Now all she had to do was wait for the Jehovah's Witnesses to make a reappearance in her neighborhood. A mission field would soon be walking right up to her own door! She could serve the Lord without even leaving her home. She was nervous, but excited.

CHAPTER 5

Ministering
on the
Doorstep

S ure enough, one morning as Beverly Williams looked out her front window, there were the Jehovah's Witnesses on her street and heading for her house.

She quickly prayed and put her Bible in a handy place. Mentally, she reviewed the hints from the cults ministries, many of whom had been Jehovah's Witnesses in the past.

Fresh in her mind was the reminder that most Jehovah's Witnesses are greeted by an unkind and irritated face, even from Christians. They are disposed of in the shortest possible time, often with rudeness or the remark, "I don't need this, I'm saved." She remembered one testimony of an ex-J.W. who said, "I really wasn't satisfied with what I had in the organization, but I wasn't going to leave and become miserable like the church-attenders I met at the door."

Beverly Williams was now keenly aware that the only Christian witness the Jehovah's Witnesses have is the Christians they meet at the doors. If they can't see Christ in the householder, they may never see Christ at all. She was determined that her relationship with Christ would shine through, no matter what was said in the encounter.

Soon her doorbell rang. As she opened the door, she had a welcoming smile, greeted the two Jehovah's Witnesses warmly, and made introductions all around. This small act of kindness put them slightly off balance, since they like to feel persecuted. However, they recovered and proceeded with their presentation.

All of the Jehovah's Witness training for the house-to-house ministry dealt with overcoming objections from the householder. They were prepared to argue or override anything the householder might say. Very soon the encounter could degenerate into an argument. The way to prevent this is for the householder to raise no objections initially.

Beverly Williams remembered her suggestions from the cult ministries well. Although she could not agree with the points raised on the "new earth" by Joe Simpson, she listened politely, and when he paused for her to object, she said instead, "Please go on," and smiled.

She listened courteously through to the end of Joe's presentation. Without interruptions it only lasted two or three minutes, and then he offered her literature.

She thanked him and said she would take the literature in a moment. She knew that if she took the literature the Jehovah's Witnesses would come back for a return visit. Also, they would not leave her doorstep until she did take their literature, since placement quotas are important to them. So she kept them there by the promise to take the current offer. Now it was her turn. She began to speak.

"You were so kind to come by and share some Scriptures from the Bible with me. I wonder if I might share one with you?"

The Jehovah's Witnesses agreed. After all, she listened to them. She knew that if one of them began to interrupt her presentation, she should say that she listened politely to them, and would they please do the same for her? She was aware that usually Jehovah's Witnesses are sent out in pairs, a strong one with a weaker or newer one. However, both seemed willing to listen this time, so she proceeded.

"You have come to my door this morning, because you really believe you are in the true faith. Is this right?"

Both Jehovah's Witnesses agreed that they were in the true faith and were doing Jehovah's will.

Beverly Williams now pointed out that there is a simple Bible test as to whether or not one is in the true faith. She turned to 2 Corinthians 13:5 (which she had previously marked in her Bible) and read:

> Test yourselves to see if you are in the faith; examine yourselves! Or do you not recognize this about yourselves, that Jesus Christ is in you—unless indeed you fail the test?

She then told the two men that she was so happy to know she passed this Bible test for being in the true faith. Sharing her testimony in a brief way, she explained how, when she was at a difficult time in her life, she had invited Jesus Christ to be Lord of her life. He had never left her since that time but was constantly with her, "in her." She knew by His indwelling presence that she was in the true faith.

The expected objection was now raised by the Jehovah's Witnesses who were following along in their altered bible, The New World Translation of the Scriptures. Joe pointed out that his Bible did not say Christ could be "*in* you," but "in union with you." He read aloud:

> Keep testing whether you are in the faith, keep proving what you yourselves are. Or do you not recognize that Jesus Christ is in union with you? Unless you are disproved (NWT).

Beverly asked Joe, "Do you have an interlinear Bible, Joe? You know, one with the Greek words above and the literal English words below?" Joe replied that he didn't have one, but he could get one at the Kingdom Hall.

Beverly then took his literature offer and set a firm time for him to return. She requested that he bring his interlinear Bible, and that he also check the original words to see if "in union with" was actually in the text, or had been added.

It is vitally important that Jehovah's Witnesses begin to question their own translation, and check it against their Kingdom Interlinear Translation, which seems harmless enough to them. However, many have been set free from the Watch Tower Society by use of this very publication which shows their additions and alterations to the text, particularly concerning Jesus Christ. If they question one Scripture to start, they will soon check other ones as well.

After they left, Beverly prayed for the Holy Spirit to convict them of the truth of the indwelling Christ and prayed over their next encounter. She prepared the Scriptures she wanted to share.

On the appointed day, Joe showed up with an experienced elder. The elders do not let their new members "go it alone" or with ordinary ones on return visits. They are very protective of their recruits. Elder Leo Stern accompanied Joe to Beverly Williams' house.

The Jehovah's Witnesses fully intended to initiate a "Bible study" using the book they left, and they intended to present their "new earth" theology, playing on the fears that most people have about world conditions.

Beverly, on the other hand, intended to let these secondary doctrines alone for the moment and concentrate on Jesus Christ. She had chosen for her first encounter the subject of whether Jesus Christ was the Archangel Michael or not. This is the best place to begin, since this doctrine can be easily proven false by the use of a few Scriptures, and Jehovah's Witnesses can "prove" this doctrine only by "comparison of Scriptures" and not by actual clear-cut texts.

Although Leo Stern tried to take control of the encounter, Beverly stopped him in his tracks by keeping the subject on what she wished to discuss, namely, "Is Jesus the Archangel Michael?"

CHAPTER 6

◆

Is Jesus Michael the Archangel?

The encounter began with Beverly asking Leo to answer a Bible question she had. The Jehovah's Witnesses are always pleased to answer questions, since they feel they have all the answers. She asked him if Jesus Christ was really Michael the Archangel. He replied that He was. She then asked him to produce one Scripture actually calling Jesus "Michael." This kept him busy so she could talk to Joe. There is no Scripture calling Jesus Christ Michael, and she had ready answers for any Scripture he might come up with.

From her research she knew that Jehovah's Witnesses have held varying views on the subject of Michael over the years. First they had Michael as the Pope of Rome, then declared emphatically that Michael was not Christ, but then did an about-face and now teach that he is Christ!

Beverly found that the following chart gave her all the information she needed to prove conclusively that Jesus Christ is not Michael the Archangel.

Beverly was not at all disturbed that Leo Stern objected vigorously to her pointing out two key Scriptures that proved Jesus was not Michael.

Leo then dragged Joe away from her house with

Is Jesus Christ
Michael the Archangel?

Scriptures Relating to Michael	Points Taught	Could This Be Jesus?
Daniel 10:13: "Michael, one of the chief princes, came to help me, for I had been left there with the Kings of Persia."	Michael is only one of several other "chief princes." He is not unique.	Jesus is never called "Chief Prince" in the Bible. It is not one of His titles. He is called, however, "King of Kings and Lord of Lords" (Revelation 19:16).
Daniel 10:21: "There is no one who stands firmly with me against these forces except Michael your prince."	Michael is portrayed as *your prince*— that is, the "prince" for the exiled nation of Israel, who fights for them. This battle is between angelic forces.	Jesus does have angelic forces with Him when He fights (see Matthew 25:31), but He is never referred to as the "Prince" of these forces, rather He is identified as "the King" (Matthew 25:34).
Daniel 12:1: "At that time Michael, the great prince who stands guard over the sons of your people, will arise."	Michael is here portrayed as a *great prince* who stands guard over Israel— obviously a guardian angel.	Jesus is never called a "great prince" in the Bible, nor a guardian. He is also never called an angel!
Revelation 12:7: "And there was war in heaven, Michael and his angels waging war with the dragon. And the dragon and his angels waged war."	Michael is fighting at the head of his angels, which is only proper, since he is a chief angel.	Revelation 12:5,6, just previous to this Scripture, portrays Christ as a "male," a "son." Verse 10 calls Him "Christ." Jesus is not called an angel in the book of Revelation.

First Thessalonians 4:16: "The Lord Himself will descend from heaven with a shout, and with the voice of the archangel, and with the trumpet of God; and the dead in Christ shall rise first."	1. The Lord Himself descends 2. "with" shouting 3. "with" the voice of the archangel 4. "with" the trumpet of God.	1. The Lord Jesus Christ is identified. 2-4. All these things are *with* Christ: "a shout," "the voice of the archangel," and "the trumpet of God." If we say this verse is saying that Jesus is an archangel because the voice of the archangel is *with Him*, then we must also say that Jesus is "a shout," "a voice," and "a trumpet"! Ridiculous!
Jude 9: "Michael the archangel, when he disputed with the devil and argued about the body of Moses, did not dare pronounce against him a railing judgment, but said, *The Lord rebuke you.*'"	1. Michael is an archangel. The New American Standard Concordance, p. 1636, lists the meaning of "archangel" as "a chief angel." This agrees with Daniel 10:13. 2. Michael did not dare to rebuke Satan. 3. Michael spoke of "the Lord" (*Kurios* in Greek) rebuking Satan.	1. Jesus is not a "chief angel," nor is He a "chief *over* the angels." 2. Whereas Michael did not have the power to rebuke Satan, Jesus rebuked Satan many times (see Matthew 17:18; Mark 9:25; etc.). Therefore Jesus is not Michael. 3. Michael referred to "the Lord" as separate from himself. "The Lord" is a New Testament reference to Jesus and an Old Testament reference to YHWH.

* Adapted from tract by Lorri MacGregor (MacGregor Ministries).

the phony excuse that they "had another appointment." She observed Joe questioning Leo on the sidewalk in front of her home and knew that Joe was upset at being made to leave. Also, Leo had failed to produce that all-important Scripture Beverly had asked for, calling Jesus "Michael."

Also, Beverly had questioned Joe about whether he had checked out the Scripture they first discussed at her door, about Christ being *"in you"* or *"in union with you."* Joe had checked his Kingdom Interlinear Bible and mentioned that the words *"in union with"* were not in the original text, but had been inserted. She was pleased to see Joe check the Scriptures she had used today in the Kingdom Interlinear.

She closed this episode with a fervent prayer for the Holy Spirit to convict Joe and Leo of what they had heard, and she prayed that Joe would have the courage to return as he had promised.

She prepared herself to discuss the deity of Jesus Christ if and when Joe returned.

CHAPTER 7

◆

Is Jesus Just "a god"?

Beverly Williams now prepared herself to deal with the deity of Jesus Christ. She knew the Jehovah's Witnesses bitterly attack the trinity, calling it a doctrine of Satan the Devil. She also knew that the trinity concept was much more complicated to deal with, and should be left to a later time. To start, she must prove out of the Bible the deity of Jesus Christ. She already had a good start by proving at the previous encounter that Jesus Christ was not Michael the Archangel. Now she wanted to correct the false concept that Jesus was only "a god."

She again reviewed the material she had on the beliefs of the Jehovah's Witnesses concerning God and Jesus Christ. She read:

Jehovah's Witnesses worship and acknowledge only one God, namely God the Father, whom they call "Jehovah." They believe the Holy Spirit is an "active force" or God's power, and they reduce Jesus to a secondary god, who is also known as the archangel Michael in their theology. They reject the trinity.

J.W. Doctrine on God

Jehovah's Witnesses are taught by the Watch

Tower Society that Almighty God Jehovah created a secondary god, Jesus Christ. To illustrate:

$$\bigcirc \quad + \quad \circ \quad = \quad 2$$

| Jehovah [One God] | + | Jesus [Secondary god] | = | Belief in *two* gods. |

Establish that there is *one true God* by nature. They will agree. Now we ask the Jehovah's Witnesses the key question: Is Jesus a true god or a false god? They will have to admit that Jesus is a true god. This forces them to believe in more than one true god! You can't believe in two true gods as the J.W.'s do and still be a Christian and a Bible believer! This is a real dilemma for Jehovah's Witnesses.

According to the Bible, there is only *one true, eternal God* by nature. All others are created, and by biblical definition, *false*.

> Turn to Me and be saved, all the ends of the earth, for I am *God*, and *there is no other* (Isaiah 45:22).

> Now to the King *eternal*, immortal, invisible, *the only God*, be honor and glory forever and ever. Amen (1 Timothy 1:17).

> God is *only one* (Galatians 3:20).

> We know that the Son of God has come and has given us understanding, in order that we might know *Him who is true*, and we

are in *Him who is true*, in His Son Jesus Christ. This is *the true God* and eternal life (1 John 5:20).

You believe that *God is one*; you do well; the demons also believe, and shudder (James 2:19).

So the Scriptures are clear: There is only one true eternal God. The words *one, true,* and *eternal* indicate that all other gods outside of this *true eternal one* must be, by biblical definition, *false*. The other gods are also not eternal, but created by someone.

The Bible acknowledges the existence of other gods, but places them in categories other than the exclusive position of the *one true God*. These *"gods"* are, without exception, *created and false*. They are not *God* by nature.

However, at that time, when you did not know God, you were slaves to those which *by nature are no gods* (Galatians 4:8).

Even if there are so-called gods whether in heaven or on earth, as indeed there are many gods and many lords, yet for us there is but *one God*, the Father, from whom are all things, and we exist for Him; and *one Lord*, Jesus Christ by whom are all things, and we exist through Him (1 Corinthians 8:5,6).

Belief in the one true God of Scripture has always necessitated renouncing all other gods. The Ten Commandments begin:

I am the Lord your God, who brought you out of the land of Egypt, out of the house of slavery. *You shall have no other gods before Me.* . . . You shall not worship them or serve them; for I, the Lord your God, am a jealous God (Exodus 20:2,3,5).

Categories of "gods" in Scripture

Category 1—Satanic

We know that we are of God, and the whole world lies in the power of the evil one (1 John 5:19).

The god of this world has blinded the minds of the unbelieving, that they might not see the light of the gospel of the glory of Christ, who is the image of God (2 Corinthians 4:4).

It is evident, if we believe Jesus to be "a god," that he would *not* fit this category!

Category 2—Idols

A. Carved idols: He did evil in the sight of the Lord as Manasseh his father had done, and Amon sacrificed to all the carved images which his father Manasseh had made, and he served them (2 Chronicles 33:22).

B. Molten images: They shall be turned back and be utterly put to shame who

> trust in idols, who say to molten images,
> "You are our gods" (Isaiah 42:17).

> Do not be idolaters (1 Corinthians 10:7).

If we think that Jesus is "a god," He would *not* fit into the above category!

Category 3—Exaltation of Humans to Gods

> Jesus answered them, "Has it not been written in your Law, 'I said, you are gods'?" (John 10:34).

Who were called "gods" by Jesus? It was the judges who ruled Israel before the days of the kings. These judges had the power of life and death over the people, and were called "gods."

Were they true gods or false gods? Psalm 82, from which Jesus was quoting, tells us in verses 1 and 2:

> God takes His stand in His own con-gregation; He judges in the midst of the rulers. How long will you judge unjustly and show partiality to the wicked?

Yes, God's judgment awaited these men–"gods":

> I said, "You are gods, and all of you are sons of the Most High. Nevertheless you will die like men" (Psalm 82:6,7).

No exalted man is a true god, but a false one. Do not be deceived by the same lie that Satan told Eve in the Garden of Eden:

You will be like God [or "as gods"],
knowing good and evil (Genesis 3:5).

The teaching that any man can become a god is unscriptural. God has an exclusive claim on god-ship.

If we think Jesus is "a god," we cannot place him in this category of corrupt men.

This concludes the biblical categories of "gods." Jesus fits *none* of them. Jesus is *not* "a god."

Support for the John 1:1 Translation

"and the Word was a god" (NWT)

The New World Translation of the Jehovah's Witnesses caused quite a stir in the religious world when the end of John 1:1 was translated "and the Word was a god."

They are not without some support for this translation, however, and we will now take a closer look at the precedents for translating "and the Word was a god."

We find this important topic discussed in the Watch Tower publication *The Word, Who Is He? According to John*. On page 5 we read:

> Similar is the reading by a former Catholic Priest: "In the beginning was the Word, and the Word was with God, and the Word was a god."

We are directed to a footnote which reads:

> *The New Testament—a New Translation and Explanation* Based on the Oldest Manuscripts, by Johannes Greber [a translation from German into English], edition of 1937, the front cover of this bound translation being stamped with a gold cross.

Likewise, we find this translation by Johannes Greber referred to in *Make Sure of All Things, Hold Fast to What Is Fine* [1965], page 489.

The Johannes Greber New Testament obviously set a precedent for the Jehovah's Witnesses, and their rendering of John 1:1 is almost identical.

We again find Johannes Greber quoted in *Aid to Bible Understanding* on pages 1134 and 1669. This translation is available from the Johannes Greber Memorial Foundation, 139 Hillside Ave., Teaneck, NJ 07666.

Prior to the introduction of this New Testament by Greber, we find the following statement about the man himself and his prayers for guidance in his translating task:

> Prayers . . . were answered, and discrepancies clarified to him, by God's Spirit World. At times he was given the correct answers in large illuminated letters and words passing before his eyes. Other times he was given the correct answers during prayer meetings. His wife, a medium of God's Spirit World, was often instrumental in conveying the correct answers from God's Messengers to Pastor Greber.

As we examine this New Testament further we find constant references to God's "holy spirits" [plural], and it becomes more and more obvious that we are dealing with a man deep into spiritism. This, of course, is forbidden by God's Word. Leviticus 19:31 says:

> Do not turn to mediums or spiritists; do not seek them out to be defiled by them.

Johannes Greber published not only the New Testament, but we are also told by his foundation:

> Late in the summer of 1923 God's holy spirits contacted Pastor Greber.... In his spare time he started to work on his book *Communication with the Spirit World of God*. Later he translated the New Testament with the help of God's spirit world.

The Johannes Greber Memorial Foundation provided a photocopy of a letter from the Watch Tower Society acknowledging receipt of not only several of his New Testaments, but also Greber's book *Communication with the Spirit World of God*.

Why has the Watch Tower Society of Jehovah's Witnesses willingly and knowingly been in communication with a spiritistic society?

It is true that in the April 1, 1983, *Watchtower*, page 31, under "Questions from the Readers," the Society claims that they found out from the 1980 edition of the New Testament by Johannes Greber that he was involved with spiritism, and therefore they would not quote from his Bible in the future.

However, the facts are that the Watch Tower Society knew, at least from 1956, that Johannes Greber was involved with demon spirits. They published an article to that effect in the *Watchtower* of February 15, 1956. With this knowledge they deliberately used his "translation" of the Bible as a basis for their New World Translation of the Holy Scriptures in 1961. These dates do not lie.

Why would the Watch Tower Society embrace a translation of John 1:1 given by demon spirits? Every Jehovah's Witness needs to check this out.

Continuing on with the precedents for translating John 1:1 "and the Word was a god," we also find the Watch Tower Society quoting on page 5 of *The Word, Who Is He? According to John*:

> This reading is also found in the *New Testament in an Improved Version*, published in London, England, in 1808.

We are directed to a footnote which reads "The title pages reads:

> The New Testament in an Improved Version, upon the basis of Archbishop Newcome's New Translation: with a Corrected Text, and Notes Critical and Explanatory. Published by a Society for Promoting Christian Knowledge and the Practice of Virtue, by the Distribution of Books—Unitarian."

Yes, the key word above is *Unitarian*. This is a cult teaching that Jesus was an extraordinarily good man, but nothing more. A Mr. Thos. Belsham (after Archbishop Newcome's death) altered his text, according to the *Historical Catalogue . . . of the English Bible*, page 334.

This altered text dishonoring Archbishop Newcome's careful scholarship also provided a basis for the New World Translation's "and the Word was a god."

Archbishop Newcome certainly never said, "The Word was 'a god.'" Why would the Watch Tower use as their guide a cult denying the biblical Christ, and be guilty of altering a reputable biblical text? Every Jehovah's Witness needs to check this out.

A third precedent for translating John 1:1 "and the Word was a god" comes from the *Emphatic Diaglott*, by Benjamin Wilson. His translation actually reads "the Logos was God," but he placed the words "a god" under *theos* in the Greek and English. Yet in the alphabetical index of the *Emphatic Diaglott* under the heading "Almighty" we find:

> ALMIGHTY. Able to do all things; an attribute of Deity; also of the glorified Jesus. Rev. 1:8.

So even the *Emphatic Diaglott*, which the Watch Tower prints on its own presses, recognizes that Jesus Christ is Almighty God, and correctly applies Revelation 1:8 to Jesus.

Furthermore, Mr. Wilson never studied biblical Greek in college. He was a follower of John Thomas, a proven false prophet by failure of his dates, and the founder of the Christadelphians, a Christ-dishonoring cult.

All the precedents for translating John 1:1 "and the Word was a god" crumble away under close and honest scholarship!

Why would the Watch Tower Society choose precedents that are false and even demonic? Why do they choose to ignore Greek scholars who are reputable? Every Jehovah's Witness needs to check this out.

Each one of us needs to settle the question "Is Jesus *the God* or merely "a god"?

If we have the right Jesus Christ, we are right for all eternity, but if we have the wrong Jesus Christ, we are wrong for all eternity.

Is Jesus "a god"? Based on the Scriptures, we answer a resounding *No*!

Jesus is not some false, created god, but is *God Almighty*! No wonder Colossians 2:9 says:

> In Him all the fullness of Deity dwells in bodily form.

All is all and full is full; Jesus is fully God!

♦

CHAPTER 8

Misrepresenting Christ in the New World Translation

As Beverly Williams continued on in her research, she prepared herself to deal with some of the distortions contained in the New World Translation published by the Jehovah's Witnesses. She marked these changed Scriptures in her own Bible so she would be alerted should Jehovah's Witnesses use them in their discussions with her. She made marginal notes right next to these Scriptures, correcting their distortions. Using her cult ministries materials as her guide, she prepared to deal with this deception.

A most revealing publication of the Watch Tower Society is an interlinear translation called *The Kingdom Interlinear Translation of the Greek Scriptures*, published in 1969. In this book their Scripture distortions can be clearly seen, especially the altering of the text in places where Jesus is called "God." So successful has this publication been in setting Jehovah's Witnesses free from the Watch Tower Society that they have taken it out of print and substituted one in which the distortions are masked much more successfully. We recommend finding the original if at all possible.

Distortion of
Colossians 2:9

Because it is in him that all the fullness of
the divine quality dwells bodily (NWT).

Notice the words "divine quality." They are found
nowhere in the Greek text. Why then are they inserted in the New World Translation? Obviously because the Jehovah's Witness leaders could not have
their membership know that *all the fullness of Deity* is
dwelling in Christ bodily! Notice the Greek/English
side of the *Kingdom Interlinear Translation*:

Because in him is dwelling down all the
fullness of the godship bodily (KIT).

Looking up the word "godship" in any reputable Bible dictionary, we find it also reads "Godhead"
or "Deity." It can never be honestly translated "divine quality." Why would the Watch Tower Translators be so dishonest as to insert extra words in the
text, and at the same time ignore the truth about
Jesus? The correct reading of Colossians 2:9 would
be:

In Him all the fullness of Deity dwells in
bodily form.

Yes, all is all, and full is full, and Jesus is Deity in
the flesh! No wonder the verse just previous, Colossians 2:8, warns us to watch out for those who
would misrepresent Christ!

Misrepresentation of Christ
by Ignoring the Context
of Scriptures

Much of J.W. doctrine is built by using the Bible like a dictionary. You choose your doctrine, and then you hunt through the pages of the Bible for a phrase here and a phrase there that will seem to support what you said. Used (or abused) this way, you can make the Bible say just about anything you want it to! Misrepresentation of Christ by ignoring the context is a favorite method of Witnesses, and we give an example here.

Presenting Jesus as a Creature, "First Created"

Since Jesus is eternal, and the Bible teaches this fact, these Scriptures are never used. The next step is to choose other Scriptures that on the surface seem to teach that Jesus is created. J.W.'s choose Proverbs 8:22,30 after telling the "Bible study" that Jesus is created. The prospect reads:

> Jehovah himself produced me as the beginning of his way, the earliest of his achievements of long ago (v. 22). Then I came to be beside him as a master worker, and I came to be the one he was specially fond of day by day, I being glad before him all the time" (v. 30 NWT).

Being "primed" in this manner, the prospect assumes that Jesus Christ is the subject of Proverbs chapter 8. However, a study *in context* reveals that the true subject of Proverbs is wisdom personified, and not Jesus Christ at all! Always check the context of the isolated verses misused by Jehovah's Witnesses.

Why not ask the Jehovah's Witness, "If Jehovah created Jesus first, and then Jesus was beside Him as a master workman for the rest of creation as you teach, could you please explain Isaiah 44:24 to me?"

> Thus says the Lord [YHWH], your Redeemer, and the one who formed you from the womb, "I the Lord [YHWH] am the maker of all things, stretching out the heavens *by myself*, and spreading out the earth *all alone*."

Misrepresenting Christ by Redefining Bible Terms

Jehovah's Witnesses give their own meanings to Bible terms. Rather than accepting true definitions which would disprove their doctrines, they invent new meanings. An example is the term "firstborn" as applied to Jesus Christ. The Witnesses attempt to use this redefined term to prove that Jesus was created first, and so is only a creature. Colossians 1:15 reads in their Bible:

> He is the image of the invisible God, the first-born of all creation (NWT).

Here the Scripture is correct, but J.W.'s read and teach it with a faulty definition. They equate "firstborn" with "first-created," as programmed by the Society.

Notice first of all that this Scripture teaches that Jesus is the *image* of the invisible God, not the *creation* of the invisible God. When we look in a mirror, what do we see? An image of ourselves. Is it us? Of course! So Christ is the *visible image* of the *invisible God*. Matthew 1:23 calls Him "God with us." Is He then God? Of course!

In this Scripture in Colossians 1:15, Jesus is also called "the firstborn of all creation." What does this mean? First of all, it does *not* mean "first-created" as the J.W.'s teach. The word in Greek for "first-created" is *protoktistos*. This term is *never* used in connection with Jesus Christ.

The term "firstborn" means in Greek *preeminence in rank*. If we continue reading in Colossians chapter 1 the meaning becomes clear. Verse 16 says:

> By Him [Christ] all things were created, both in the heavens and on earth, visible and invisible, whether thrones or dominions or rulers or authorities—all things have been created by Him and for Him.

Verse 17 continues:

> He is before all things, and in Him all things hold together.

We rest our case. Jesus Christ is *"before all things."* This means that before the heavens and the earth, before the angels, before the creation of man, Christ is the Creator, the one preeminent in rank, the first-born of all creation.

Additional Tampering Necessary to Support the Distortions

It was necessary for the translators of the New World Translation to further alter Colossians chapter 1 to hide the fact that Jesus is the Creator. They dishonestly inserted the word "other" four times in verses 16 and 17 to prop up their false doctrine that Jesus is a creature.

Micah 5:2 says of Christ:

> His goings forth are from long ago, from the days of eternity.

The Hebrew word here for "eternity" is *olam*. No creature is ever described with this word—only God. It is used of YHWH (Jehovah) in Psalm 90:2. God is eternal.

Redefining "Only-Begotten"

Jehovah's Witnesses teach that Jesus was "only-begotten" when Jehovah supposedly created Him in the beginning. Once again, this term has no reference to any so-called creation, and Acts 13:33 even applies this term to the time of Christ's resurrection:

> God has fulfilled this promise to our children in that *He raised up Jesus*, as it is also written in the second Psalm, *"Thou art my Son; today I have begotten Thee."*

Redefining "Beginning of the Creation of God"

Jehovah's Witnesses quote one phrase of Revelation 3:14:

> . . . the beginning of the creation of God (NWT).

This one phrase now becomes a proof text that Jesus was created. However, a perusal of several reputable Greek dictionaries produced these definitions for "Beginning": "Supervisor," "Designer," "Cause," "Origin," and "Source." Obviously, in context, Jesus is the Creator.

Refusing to Translate Words with Their Primary Meaning

Why would Jehovah's Witness leaders translate the same Greek word as "worship" when it applied to the Father and then change it to "obeisance" when it applied to the Son? Simply because they do not want their followers to worship Jesus, for worship belongs to God alone. Followers are then further misled by being told that "obeisance" is not really worship.

Reputable Bibles read in Matthew 28:9:

> And behold, Jesus met them and greeted them. And they came up and took hold of His feet and worshiped Him.

If the disciples as Jews who believed in worshiping God alone worshiped Jesus, then we should follow their example, recognizing Him as God and worshiping Him also.

Figuratizing the Second Coming of Christ

When Christ failed to show up in person first in 1874 and then in 1914, the dates set by the Jehovah's Witnesses for His visible second coming and the termination of the world, rather than admit their error and repent they invented a new doctrine. Scriptures dealing with the visible second coming of Christ were figuratized or spiritualized. This way they could claim that Christ did come in 1914, but was conveniently invisible!

Matthew 24:3 was altered to read:

> What will be the sign of your presence and of the conclusion of the system of things? (NWT).

Altering "coming" to "presence" solved one problem in their false prophecy, but what were they to do with Revelation 1:7?

> Look! He is coming with the clouds, and every eye will see him, and those who pierced him; and all the tribes of the earth will beat themselves in grief because of him. Yes, Amen (NWT).

Why would this Scripture bother saying "Look!" if we couldn't see Him? The embarrassing phrase "every eye will see him" had to be figuratized to mean "eyes of understanding" acquired upon believing Watch Tower publications. Why then is the Greek word for "eye" the same as for the "eyes" that Jesus gave sight to when healing a blind person (Matthew 20:34)? Jesus healed *literal* eyes.

We might also ask, how exactly will "those who pierced Him" see Him, when Witnesses teach a soul-sleep/annihilation for the dead instead of the Bible teaching of a conscious existence after death?

The altering of Bible texts to try to harmonize them with one's false doctrines presents a never-ending web of deceit.

Challenge the Witnesses to believe the Bible exactly as it is written!

Old Testament Changes

In the New World Translation, the Jehovah's Witnesses have translated Zechariah 12:10 this way:

> They will certainly look to the One whom they pierced through (NWT).

In this Scripture Jehovah (YHWH) Himself is speaking, and reliable translations read correctly:

> They will look on *Me* whom they have pierced.

Yes, *Jehovah God Himself* says He was pierced through for our transgressions. The Watch Tower Society could not have their followers knowing that Jesus is Jehovah, and so they altered this text. However, they overlooked altering the Scripture that has

Jehovah telling us He was sold for 30 pieces of silver, so here it is. It begins with Zechariah speaking:

> Then I said to them: "If it is good in *your* eyes, give [me] my wages; but if not, refrain." And they proceeded to pay my wages, thirty pieces of silver. At that Jehovah said to me: "Throw it to the treasury—that majestic value with which I have been valued from their standpoint. Accordingly I took the thirty pieces of silver and threw it into the treasury at the house of Jehovah" (Zechariah 11:12,13 NWT).

Yes, it was *Jehovah God Himself* who was valued and sold for 30 pieces of silver and pierced through for our transgressions, according to His own words. John 19:37 directly applies this Zechariah prophecy to Jesus Christ.

The Watch Tower Society also had to alter Acts 20:28 to read:

> Shepherd the congregation of God, which he purchased with the blood of his own (Son) (NWT).

Notice the inserted word (Son), which is not found in any Greek text. It is an addition to suit Watch Tower doctrine. The Scripture in a reliable Bible reads:

> Shepherd the church of God, which He purchased with His own blood.

This instruction to the elders was plain enough. It was God's own blood which purchased the church, and any so-called "shepherds" not teaching this truth are simply not true shepherds.

The "Taking in Knowledge" Distortion of John 17:3

Jehovah's Witness leaders needed a Scripture to promote their "Bible studies," which are really studies of their own literature, so they altered John 17:3 to provide one:

> This means everlasting life, their *taking in knowledge* of you, the only true God, and of the one whom you sent forth, Jesus Christ (NWT).

The friendly Witness at your door will then explain that you must *"take in knowledge"* from their organization to have salvation through the dreadful "battle of Armageddon" coming soon.

This Scripture really reads:

> This is eternal life, that they may *know Thee*, the only true God, and Jesus Christ whom Thou hast sent.

Yes, eternal life comes from *knowing God personally*, in the Person of Jesus Christ. A constant studying of Scripture is a good thing, but "taking in knowledge" of itself will not give us eternal life. Jesus Himself stressed this point in John 5:39,40:

> You search the Scriptures because you think that in them you have eternal life; and it is these that bear witness of Me; and you are unwilling to come to Me that you may have life.

No organization can give salvation. One *Watchtower* headlined, *"Come to Jehovah's Organization for Salvation,"* but in fact salvation is only in Jesus Christ, not in any organization.

Beverly Williams closed her Bible with a sigh. She had spent several days marking these Scriptures, cross-referencing them, and making notes in her Bible margins.

Now she had answers for the Jehovah's Witness claims that Jesus was only "a god," should the need arise to defend Him against these errors.

She hoped, however, that she could proceed directly with proving Christ's deity from the Bible on the next call. As things worked out, she was able to proceed directly without needing most of this background information, yet she was glad she was prepared for any occurrence, and she felt a real sense of satisfaction from the work of preparation.

She hoped and prayed that Joe would return as he had arranged, and that Elder Leo had not forbidden him to see her. She prayed that the Holy Spirit was even now convicting Joe about Jesus.

CHAPTER 9

✦

Presenting the Deity of Jesus Christ

B everly Williams found new meaning in so many Scriptures, now that she had started studying them with a view to correcting Jehovah's Witness doctrines concerning Christ. This one became a particular favorite to her:

> Sanctify Christ as Lord in your hearts, always being ready to make a defense to everyone who asks you to give an account for the hope that is in you, yet with gentleness and reverence (1 Peter 3:15).

She knew that if she hoped to effectively win souls for Christ out of the cults, she must be ready to defend the deity of Christ above all else, for Christ is always misrepresented by the cult groups. This misrepresentation usually takes the form of denying His deity. In the world of the cults, she now knew, they either deified man or humanized God. She was determined as a Christian to present them with the right Jesus Christ, since they have "another Jesus" (2 Corinthians 11:4).

She reviewed a suggested presentation one more time.

Presenting the True
Jesus Christ

The Jesus Christ of the Bible is truly God but also truly man, and both these aspects need to be dealt with in order to clear up the confusion in the cultists' minds.

In our human thinking, which is finite, we cannot always understand the infinite God. However, He has revealed Himself through the pages of the Bible, and we must either accept the revelation of Himself that He has made or else resort to manmade doctrines and concepts. Most cults will accept the Bible as an authority, so we may proceed.

Believing John 1:1 as Written

In the beginning was the Word, and the Word was with God, and the Word was God.

In our human thinking we may say, "Wait a minute, how can the Word be *with* God and yet *be* God, since there is only *one God*?" Our human understanding is just not up to this statement. We know that *we* can't be "with" someone and yet "be" that someone, but remember, God does not have our limitations! God reveals Himself this way throughout Scripture. An example is Isaiah 44:6:

Thus says the Lord [YHWH], the King of Israel and his Redeemer, the Lord [YHWH] of Hosts [sounds like two, but...], "I am the first and I am the last, and there is no God besides Me."

We must either accept this truth or reject it. Let's choose to accept the fact that God says there is only one God, and that the "Word was God." This is what the early church did, although they did not fully understand it. We find what I like to call an early creed of the church, a common confession, in 1 Timothy 3:16:

> By common confession great is the *mystery* of godliness: God who was revealed in the flesh, was vindicated in the Spirit, beheld by angels, proclaimed among the nations, believed on in the world, taken up in glory.

Knowing God's Mystery, Jesus Christ

Just because Jesus Christ is called a "mystery," this doesn't mean that we can never know Him or understand how He can be truly God and truly man at the same time. Colossians 2:2 promises:

> . . . that their hearts may be encouraged, having been knit together in love, and attaining to all the wealth that comes from the full assurance of understanding, resulting in a *true knowledge* of God's mystery, that is, Christ Himself.

Jesus Christ Is Almighty God

We need to make the vital point that *Jesus Christ is Almighty God* at the very beginning. He is not some secondary god, or one of many gods, but He really is the *one true Almighty God*. Christians believe that Jesus Christ is Almighty God manifest in the flesh. What follows is a good presentation to Jehovah's Witnesses, Mormons, and others denying the full deity of Jesus Christ.

"The First and the Last"
Presentation

I title this presentation on the deity of Christ "The First and the Last," not only because it uses this term but also because it uses the first and last chapters of Revelation to prove the point. We begin by reading Revelation 1:8:

> "I am the *Alpha and the Omega*," says the Lord God, "who is and who was and who is to come, the *Almighty*."

This Scripture teaches us a few points. The "Alpha and Omega" is the "Lord God Almighty," and He is coming.

All will agree, but the Witnesses will point out that their Bible inserts "Jehovah" for "Lord." Refer them to their *Kingdom Interlinear Translation* so they can see for themselves that "Jehovah" is not in the Greek text, but is an insertion by the translators of their Bible. In spite of this, all can agree that Almighty God calls Himself "The Alpha and the Omega."

Turn now to Revelation chapter 22. There are several speakers in this chapter, but we want to single out the "Alpha and Omega" speaker to see what else He has to say. Insist on reading the verses *in context*. The Speaker does not change between verses 12 and 16, so let's consider Revelation 22:12-16:

> Behold, I am coming quickly, and My reward is with Me, to render to every man according to what he has done. I am the *Alpha and the Omega, the first and the last*, the beginning and the end. Blessed are those who wash their robes, that they may have the right to the tree of life, and may enter by the gates into the city. Outside are the dogs and the sorcerers and the immoral persons and the murderers and the idolaters, and everyone who loves and practices lying. I, *Jesus*, have sent My angel to testify to you these things for the churches. I am the root and the offspring of David, the bright morning star.

Only now, with verse 17, does the Speaker change. Therefore the same Speaker, namely the Alpha and Omega, has said *all* the above things. He is "coming quickly"; He is the "Alpha and the Omega"; He is the "first and the last"; and He identifies Himself as "I, Jesus." The apostle John evidently agrees, for in verse 20 he records:

> He who testifies to these things says, "Yes, I am coming quickly." Amen. Come, Lord Jesus.

Jehovah's Witnesses will become agitated at this point, insisting that verse 12 is probably Jesus, then verse 13 must be Jehovah, then verse 16 is Jesus again. Rather than arguing, ask them, "Do you agree that in verse 13 the 'Alpha and Omega' calls Himself 'The first and the last'? They must agree. Remark that Revelation chapter 1 leaves us in no doubt as to the identity of "The first and the last." Turn to Revelation 1:13-18. This account is a vision of the "Son of man." Ask them who this is. They will reply "Jesus." You will agree. You could take the time to read through the vision, but concentrate on verses 17 and 18, where the apostle John says:

> When I saw Him, I fell at His feet as a dead man. And He laid His right hand upon me, saying, "Do not be afraid; *I am the first and the last*, and the living One, and *I was dead*, and behold I am alive forevermore, and I have the keys of death and of Hades."

Jesus has here called Himself "The first and the last," the same as He did in Revelation 22:13, where He also called Himself the "Alpha and the Omega." It is obviously Jesus speaking also in Revelation 1:8, where He repeats that He is the "Alpha and the Omega," and that He is "Almighty God." We will read Revelation 1:8 again to fully establish the claims of Jesus Christ:

> "I am the Alpha and the Omega," says the Lord God [Jesus Christ], "who is and who was and who is to come, the Almighty."

Jesus Christ is truly Almighty God by His own witness of the fact. Therefore He is not some secondary god, or one god among many, or the Archangel Michael, or only a good man. *Jesus Christ is Almighty God manifest in the flesh.*

What About the *Ho Theos* Argument?

Ho Theos means "The God" in Greek, and Jehovah's Witnesses claim that this can only be Jehovah God. We therefore refer them to the following Scriptures, and ask them to check them out in their *Kingdom Interlinear Translation.* In each case Jesus Christ is called *Ho Theos,* "The God."

Prophecy called Jesus "The God" (Matthew 1:23).

The disciples called Jesus "The God" (John 20:25-28).

The Father called Jesus "The God" (Hebrews 1:8).

Jesus Is "The God with Us"

Jesus Christ is Almighty God (Revelation 1:8), The God (Scriptures above), the True God (1 John 5:20), and the Only God. First Timothy 1:16,17 reads:

> For this reason I found mercy, in order that in me as the foremost, *Jesus Christ* might demonstrate His perfect patience, as an example for those who would believe in Him for eternal life. Now to the King *eternal*, immortal, invisible, *the only God*, be honor and glory forever and ever, Amen.

Yes, Jesus Christ is eternal (not created), and He is called "The only God." Point out the location of the "Amen" in these Scriptures. J.W.'s would like verse 16 to be Jesus but verse 17 to be Jehovah. Not possible. There were no chapter and verse divisions in the early manuscripts, and the "Amen" closes the thought. Furthermore, the subject is Jesus Christ.

There is only one true God in Scripture. He has revealed Himself in the Person of the Father, YHWH (mistranslated "Jehovah"), and in the Person of the Son, Jesus Christ. He has also revealed Himself in the Person of the Holy Spirit, but we are not dealing with that subject at this time, but with the deity of Jesus Christ.

Beverly was delighted when Joe showed up again, but with a different elder, who seemed even more hostile and rude. Nevertheless, Beverly was able to effectively do the "first and the last" presentation she had learned, and was also able to share a couple of Scriptures calling Jesus "God."

Even though Joe was forced to leave her home for a second time, she knew he was under conviction concerning Christ.

Beverly had no way of knowing that God was working in other ways in his life as well. His separated wife, Brenda, had found the Lord and had written to him about it. She had even been in touch with some cults ministries and had information on the false prophecies of Jehovah's Witnesses. She had written to Joe asking for a reconciliation.

Joe was called before the congregation committee and disciplined for going to Beverly Williams' house the second time. The elder had reported on the encounter and Joe's "rebellious attitude" in refusing to leave. Joe was threatened with disfellowshiping if he persisted in talking to Mrs. Williams. He felt like a coward as he meekly gave in to their demands. He was forced to swallow his objections and questions. He was very uncomfortable in the presence of the elders. It was one thing to be encouraged and befriended by them, but quite another experience to be chastised.

Nevertheless, Joe asked their advice about a reconciliation with Brenda, reading them her letter about her rebirth in Christ and her love for him. To his dismay, they forbade a reconciliation. They realized that she would not become a Jehovah's Witness, and neither was she just a worldly person who would not interfere with Joe's religious activities. She was the one thing the elders could not tolerate: a blood-washed, Bible-believing Christian who would want the same for Joe. Joe fled the meeting in great turmoil of mind and spirit.

On the way home, Joe felt like he had been kicked by a mule! He felt in his heart that he had done nothing wrong by discussing the Bible with Mrs. Williams. He couldn't understand the elders' dislike of her, since she only spoke out of the Bible.

Most of all, he could not understand their attitude toward Brenda. He had avoided all the advances of the sisters at the Kingdom Hall, and refused to consider divorce, just in the hopes that Brenda would forgive him and return to him. Now she was willing to do just that, and the elders asked him to abandon his fondest dreams. He just could not let go. He said aloud, "I wish Brenda were here right now."

As he pulled into his driveway, he noticed that the lights were on, and upon entering the house he was greeted by his daughter Lisa rushing into his arms, followed shortly by Brenda. Despite the elders, he was only too happy to welcome them back.

The next morning he was a troubled man. Real fear rose up in his heart over facing the elders with what he had done. He had deliberately gone against their express instructions. He had never disobeyed them before, and he knew he was in big trouble.

Brenda encouraged him to go over some of the material she had secured, and he was very troubled as he read about one hundred years of false prophecies by the Society. He could see what Jesus meant to Brenda. While she could share her born-again experience with him, she was not equipped to use her Bible to set him free from false J.W. doctrine.

Joe mentioned how he wished to speak to Beverly Williams again, but how he had promised his elders he would not go to her house again.

Brenda solved the dilemma by suggesting that they invite Beverly to their home.

When Beverly's phone rang inviting her over, she had a time of rejoicing and prayer. Joe mentioned to her that he still had questions about Jesus being inferior, so she knew just how to prepare for the upcoming encounter. She also knew she had a kindred spirit in Brenda, and that she was now not the only one praying for Joe.

CHAPTER 10

Explaining the Humanity of Jesus Christ

Beverly again prepared to minister from the Scriptures by studying ahead of time, marking her Bible, and praying before the encounter. She presented the following information to both Joe and Brenda.

Understanding Jesus' Humanity
As Well As His Deity

Jesus is truly God, but He is also truly man. Cult groups misuse the Scriptures on the subject of Jesus' humanity by attempting to apply them to the subject of His deity. This is why it is so important to always keep Scriptures in their setting.

John 1:14 says, "The Word became flesh and dwelt among us." Yes, the Word who was God came down to this earth, but why, and for how long? Hebrews 2:9 answers:

> We do see Him who has been made for a little while lower than the angels, namely, Jesus, because of the suffering of death crowned with glory and honor, that by the grace of God He might taste death for everyone.

So this humanity, this humility of Jesus was to be *"for a little while,"* and He would "taste death for everyone."

Jesus' Humanity
Explained in Philippians

Verses 5 and 6 of Philippians chapter 2 describe the humanity of Jesus:

> Have this attitude in yourselves which was also in Christ Jesus, who, although He existed in the form of God, did not regard equality with God a thing to be grasped.

The phrase "existed in the form of God" means literally in the Greek He "never ceased being in the form of God." Remembering this point, we continue to the phrase:

> [He] did not regard equality with God a thing to be grasped.

The cults love to disregard the first phrase and seize on the second to try to prove Jesus inferior. However, in context, Jesus Christ never ceased being God, but rather than grasping after the equality that was His, He chose a course of humanity and humility. Verses 7 and 8 of Philippians chapter 2 continue on:

> ...but emptied Himself, taking the form of a bondservant, and being made in the likeness of men. And being found in appearance *as a man*, He humbled Himself by

becoming obedient to the point of death, even death on a cross.

As a Man, Did Jesus Lose His Deity?

The answer to the above question is "Never!" Jesus Christ was not just a good man, as some cults teach, but was God manifest in the flesh. He did function as a man while on earth, but He was also fully God. Colossians 2:8,9 warns that false teachers would deceive people on this very point, as do the J.W.'s:

> See to it that no one takes you captive through philosophy and empty deception, according to the tradition of men, according to the elementary principles of the world rather than according to Christ. For in *Him all the fulness of deity dwells in bodily form.*

All is all, and full is full, and all the fullness of deity is dwelling in Christ *in the flesh.*

Why Did Jesus Become a Man?

This was the only way mankind could be redeemed, because of God's perfect justice. Under the Old Law Covenant it was "an eye for an eye" and "a tooth for a tooth." So also, since Adam, a perfect man, lost eternal life for us, Jesus Christ, a perfect man, could redeem it back. Romans 5:12,15 explains:

Therefore, just as through *one man* sin entered into the world, and death through sin, and so death spread to all men, because all sinned. . . . But the free gift is not like the transgression. For if by the transgression of the one the many died, much more did the grace of God and the gift by the grace of the *one Man*, Jesus Christ, abound to the many.

Truly Jesus Christ, "God with us," did function as a man on earth. He performed His miracles in the power of the Holy Spirit, and promised His disciples, "The works that I do shall he do also; and greater works than these shall he do" (John 14:12).

The disciples were mere men empowered by the Holy Spirit, and yet were promised that they could carry on as Jesus did. Jesus truly functioned as a man while on earth, fulfilling all the requirements to redeem us from Adam's sin.

Did Jesus Ever Say He Was Inferior to the Father?

The cult groups denying the deity of Jesus Christ always use Scriptures from the time of His humanity and try to apply them to His deity. A favorite example is John 14:28, quoting Jesus:

The Father is greater than I.

Is Jesus saying He is inferior to the Father? No, because if Jesus had wanted to say He was inferior,

He would have said, "The Father is *better* than I." The Greek word for "better" means "higher in nature." Jesus did not use that word, since He is not inferior to or lower in nature than the Father, as the cults teach.

Jesus used the Greek word for "greater," which means "higher in position." While Jesus was humbled, emptied, functioning as a man, the Father was in a higher position. This would be much like the president and vice-president of a company. The president is in a higher position than the vice-president, but by nature they are both men and equal.

At this point the J.W.'s will probably ask how Jesus could be on earth as "God with us" and the Father could be in heaven, also as God. Jesus even prayed to the Father while on earth. The answer is found in Isaiah 55:9:

> As the heavens are higher than the earth,
> so are My ways higher than your ways, and
> My thoughts than your thoughts.

Luke 1:37 agrees:

> Nothing will be impossible with God.

We should never try to limit God to our human understanding. If God chooses to be manifest on earth as Jesus Christ, and at the same time be in heaven as the Father, He can do anything He wants to do! "God is spirit" (John 4:24), and does not have our limitations.

Jesus' Claims While on Earth

For this cause therefore the Jews were seeking all the more to kill Him, because He not only was breaking the Sabbath, but also was calling God His own Father, *making Himself equal with God* (John 5:18).

"I and the Father are one." The Jews took up stones again to stone Him. Jesus answered them, "I showed you many good works from the Father; for which of them are you stoning Me?" The Jews answered Him, "For a good work we do not stone You, but for blasphemy; and because You, being a man, make *yourself out to be God*" (John 10:30-33).

If Jesus had been claiming to be only "a god," as J.W.'s and others teach, then He would not have been charged with blasphemy. Jesus knew He was God, His disciples worshiped Him, eyewitnesses testified to His claims to be God, and the whole church believed Acts 20:28, which tells the elders:

Be on guard for yourselves and for all the flock, among which the Holy Spirit has made you overseers, to shepherd the church of *God*, which *He purchased with His own blood*.

While He was on earth, Jesus was subject (not inferior) to His heavenly Father, and this subjection or submission appears to continue until the full establishment of the new heavens and new earth. Subject, *yes*; inferior, *no*!

Jesus Calls Himself the "I AM"

In the Gospel of John, chapter 8, we find Jesus disputing with the religious leaders. He spoke of knowing Abraham:

> The Jews therefore said to Him, "You are not yet fifty years old, and have You seen Abraham?" Jesus said to them, "Truly, truly, I say to you, before Abraham was born, I AM." Therefore they picked up stones to throw at Him; but Jesus hid Himself and went out of the temple (John 8:57-59).

Why were the Jews so angry and ready to stone Jesus? It was because He took the memorial name of God to all generations and applied it to Himself. Those Jews knew very well the account in Exodus chapter 3, where Moses was about to go in before Pharaoh, and was in dialogue with God:

> Then Moses said to God, "Behold, I am going to the sons of Israel, and I shall say to them, 'The God of your fathers has sent me to you.' Now they may say to me, 'What is His name?' What shall I say to them?" And God said to Moses, "I AM WHO I AM"; and He said, "Thus you shall say to the sons of Israel, 'I AM has sent me to you'" (Exodus 3:13,14).

Here we find a plain answer to a plain question. Moses asked God's name, and God said it was "I AM." God then went on to reveal a second name, "YHWH." He concluded the giving of both names by saying:

> This is My name forever, and this is My memorial-name to all generations (Exodus 3:15).

Jesus used the first-revealed name in John 8:58, declaring that He was the "I AM." How important is it that we believe Jesus' statement concerning His identity? John 8:24 in the original Greek tells us:

> I said therefore to you, that you shall die in your sins; for *unless you believe that I AM He*, you shall die in your sins.

We must believe that Jesus is the I AM or Deity, or we will die in our sins, without salvation. The leaders of the Jehovah's Witnesses have extensively distorted their Bible in these key areas. It is vitally important that Christians be able to defend the deity of Jesus Christ to the cults.

The Faithful Finish of Jesus' Earthly Life

> Therefore also God highly exalted Him, and bestowed on Him the name which is above every name, that at the name of Jesus every knee should bow, of those who are in heaven, and on earth, and under

the earth, and that every tongue should con-
fess that Jesus Christ is Lord, to the glory of
God the Father (Philippians 2:9-11).

Yes, Jesus is exalted in the heavens, having per-
fectly redeemed us. In heaven, on earth, and under
the earth, every knee shall bow in worship to Jesus
Christ. I tell the Jehovah's Witnesses, "You can
either worship Jesus now *willingly* in the day of
salvation, or you will worship Him *unwillingly* in the
day of judgment. Do not refuse Jesus the worship
He is due as God!

In Conclusion

We need to rise to the defense of our Lord and
Savior, Jesus Christ, who is truly God and truly
man. We need to tell the cults with the authority
of God's Word behind us that Jesus Christ is not
any kind of a "secondary god," or the "archangel
Michael," or "merely a good man." Jesus Christ is
the *only* mediator between God and man. We close
with Acts 4:12:

> There is salvation in no one else, for
> there is no other name under heaven that
> has been given among men, by which we
> must be saved.

Joe and Brenda eagerly accepted this information. Joe could now see clearly that he had been
misled about the Person of Jesus Christ by the Jehovah's Witnesses.

Beverly was thrilled to see him set aside his New
World Translation and use grandma's King James

Bible, as well as a more modern translation, the New American Standard Bible. Joe was washing out the false doctrine with the water of the Word. He was opening his heart to a relationship with the living Savior.

After Beverly left and Brenda and Lisa were in bed, Joe offered up a heartfelt prayer of repentance to God and invited Jesus to be the Lord of his life. He felt the fear of the elders lift as he prayed for Jesus to help him face them, and he knew he was no longer alone, for he now had the help of the Holy Spirit.

Joe was determined to now make a careful examination of the Watch Tower Society. He was very fond of Leo, who was like a father to him. His employer was a Jehovah's Witness, so he knew the decision he had made for Christ would cost him his livelihood.

He also wanted to have an honorable leave-taking of the Watch Tower Society. He was grateful that among the material Brenda had gotten there was a sample letter outlining how one could "disassociate" himself from the Jehovah's Witnesses.

Joe knew that if he did not take this step, the elders would disfellowship him as an "apostate" and the congregation would never understand that his reasons for leaving were his own.

He wanted to write a letter giving full and complete reasons for his disassociation. He intended to uplift Jesus Christ to His proper position, pointing out all the Scriptures he had found with Mrs. Williams' help. He intended to share his surrender to Christ and the precious truth that Jesus was "in him," and so he did pass the Bible test for a Christian at last.

He also intended to list the false prophecies and cover-ups he had researched. He would be ready for the inevitable visit from the elders!

CHAPTER 11

History of the Watch Tower Society

J oe began an in-depth study of the history of the Jehovah's Witnesses, examining photocopies of their early works provided by the cults ministries. He was appalled at what he found. He had often heard "Pastor" Russell spoken of with a reverence reserved for the apostles. He was told that Charles Taze Russell was the one appointed by God to be in charge of His affairs. Now he read the bald-faced truth from information that Brenda had obtained. One booklet was packed with interesting facts about the organization's beginnings. He read as follows.

Pagan Roots of
Jehovah's Witnesses

We must, of course, examine their founder Charles Taze Russell, and see if we can find any pagan roots.

The *Watchtower* of July 15, 1950, page 212, makes the following revealing statement about their founder:

> In his teens Charles Taze Russell, the editor, had been a member of the Congregational Church and a strong believer in the eternal torture of damned human souls

in a hell of literal fire and brimstone.... But when trying to reclaim an acquaintance, an infidel, to Christianity, he himself was routed from his sectarian position and driven into scepticism.

Hungrily he began investigating the heathen religions in search of the truth on God's purpose and man's destiny. Proving all these religions unsatisfactory and before giving up religious investigation altogether, he took up the search of the Holy Scriptures from a sceptic's viewpoint, now untrammeled by the false religious doctrines of the sectarian systems of Christendom.

What an admission! He knew so little of the Christian faith and what the Bible taught that an infidel drove him into skepticism! Not only that, but he filled his mind with pagan, occult beliefs before returning as an obviously last choice to the Bible.

Notice that his approach to the Holy Scriptures was as a skeptic, not a believer, feeling that he was free from the influence of "Christendom." I'll say he was! His mind was not protected by sound doctrine, and his head was full of the pagan, occult teaching he had so eagerly sought. It will become more and more apparent as we pursue the pagan roots of the Jehovah's Witnesses that he retained that pagan influence, all the while professing to be an unspotted Christian.

Readers of the very first issue of *Zion's Watch Tower* should have been alerted to his intentions to fuse the occult with Christianity when he stated: "A truth presented by Satan himself is just as true as a truth stated by God," and "Accept truth wherever you find it."

In his personal life Charles Taze Russell was greatly influenced by a prevailing health treatment. Various psychics professed to give "readings" by examining the bumps on one's head. This is certainly not a Christian practice, and in fact leaves one open for spiritistic influence.

He was already supposed to be dispensing Bible truth when he was, at the same time, obviously concerned with the shape of one's skull. During this time he taught in the *Watchtowers* of March 15, 1913, and January 15, 1912, that one's desire to worship God was due to the shape of one's brain. He also felt that if a dog's head was shaped like a man's, the dog would think as a man! Phrenology is not Christianity, yet he attempted to fuse the two beliefs.

Pagan Symbols on
Watch Tower Publications

If one examines Russell's theology in his series of books called *Studies in the Scriptures* he will notice a blatantly occult symbol adorning the covers. The winged solar disk is a symbol of ancient Egypt representing the sun god. Throughout the centuries it came to represent various other pagan deities. It was, in fact, the symbol for the Baal gods during Jezebel's time. Russell attempted to fuse paganism and Christianity and pass it off as untainted Christianity.

It is interesting to note that even the Watch Tower Society admits that it was a fear of hellfire that drove a young Charles Russell to seek an alternate faith.

Although the Society denied writing a biography of their founder, they in fact wrote three, in 1925, 1926, and 1927.

The Watch Tower Society has a history of lying, not only to outsiders, but to its own members! Is this Christian or pagan? The Society tries to make it Christian by calling it "justified lying." This doctrine is still in place down to our day.

We have just considered an example where they denied writing a biography of Charles Russell, but really wrote three. This doesn't fit their definition of "justified lying," which is also called "theocratic war strategy." Justified lying is defined by them as follows:

> As a soldier of Christ he is in theocratic warfare and he must exercise added caution when dealing with God's foes. Thus the Scriptures show that for the purpose of protecting the interests of God's cause, it is proper to hide the truth from God's enemies (*Watchtower*, June 1, 1960, page 352).

We will consider more of this practice of lying later, but for now will quote Revelation 22:15:

> Outside are the dogs and the sorcerers and the immoral persons and the murderers and the idolaters, and everyone who loves and practices lying.

While on the biblical subject of sorcerers, let's also look at Charles Taze Russell and sorcery. Sorcery is defined as "Divination by the assistance or supposed assistance of evil spirits; magic enchantment; witchcraft." Sorcerers are usually into astrology as well, looking for patterns and meanings in the stars. Charles Taze Russell was no exception.

In the discourse called "The Divine Plan of the Ages with Stellar Correspondencies" by Grant Jolly, a contemporary of Charles Taze Russell, we find the Society trying to foist the pagan zodiac on its followers. In this discourse, under the heading "The Heavens Declare the Glory of God," we find this statement:

> From this we may suppose that the signs [the constellations] of the Zodiac are approximately as old as the human race and perhaps of Divine origin. . . . Indeed the same Bible which points to the Great Pyramid points also to the Heavens as declaring the wonderful plan of salvation. . . . In them [that is, the stars] there is written the hope of eternal life, which God that cannot lie promised before the world began (Titus 1:2). This promise was indeed recorded in the stars before this world began.
>
> In considering the Zodiac, it will be necessary to carefully avoid the many errors that have attached themselves in connection with the various heathen religions.

What double-talk! The Society takes a completely pagan concept, embraces it, adopts it, and goes so far as to compare Jesus Christ to Pisces, even saying:

> ... Pisces shall have completely bruised the serpent's head.

The discourse would have done better to have quoted Isaiah 47:13,14 to their eager listeners:

> Let now the astrologers, those who prophesy by the stars, those who predict by the new moons, stand up and save you from what will come upon you. Behold, they have become like stubble, fire burns them; they cannot deliver themselves from the power of the flame.

Actually, much of what the early Watch Tower Society was involved in could be better called "numerology." Numerology is defined in the dictionary as "belief in the occult influence of numbers upon the life of an individual."

The *Watchtower* taught for many years that the numbers contained in the Great Pyramid foretold all kinds of events for the human race. They carefully applied every measurement, and translated it into years, months, and days. It is too complex to go into in great detail, so we will consider only one example.

The *Watchtower* of June 15, 1922, page 187, supported their "absolute date" of 539 B.C. by allowing "an inch for a year" in the Great Pyramid of Gizeh.

All their other dates are based on this so-called "absolute year" date down till today, and it is false!

This fact sets off a whole string of equally false dates. The year 607 B.C. for the desolation of Jerusalem, as used by Jehovah's Witnesses, is therefore likewise false. The "seven times" or "Gentile times" used by the Jehovah's Witnesses and calculated as 2520 years is also incorrect and without biblical basis. Their "keystone year" of 1914, originally set by pyramid calculations, is likewise in error. It will soon be evident to all Jehovah's Witnesses when the generation of 1914 passes on with no fulfillment of their hopes for a new order to be ushered in.

Every Jehovah's Witness should visit a public library and read up on pyramidology. They will discover the occult roots of their group and also be surprised to find out how many outright occult, pagan groups also name 1914 due to pyramid studies.

Modern Jehovah's Witnesses may be surprised to know that Charles Taze Russell wrapped himself in a toga (a pagan Roman garment) prior to his death, and was buried under a pyramid displaying a cross, a crown, and an open Bible, the exact symbol of the Freemasons! Even in his death he left a memorial of his attempt to fuse paganism with Christianity. Jehovah's Witnesses may visit his gravesite for themselves and see.

How sad that the Jehovah's Witnesses are following a false organization, using false dates, and built on false promises. We need to do everything in our power as concerned Christians to make them aware of this deception.

Angels Give Light
to the Society

Jehovah's Witnesses claim that they receive "angelic direction" for their activities.

Their writings from the 1930's are rampant with references to "angelic direction." We will consider just a few.

First we must explain that they give their own meaning to the biblical term "remnant," whom they consider to be their special "governing body" chosen from those 144,000 members who have a heavenly hope. This "remnant" rules from Brooklyn, New York.

Vindication, volume III, 1932, page 250, reads:

> . . . the heavenly messengers or angels of the Lord now used by the Lord in behalf of the remnant. These angels are invisible to human eyes and are there to carry out the orders of the Lord. No doubt they first hear the instruction which the Lord issues to his remnant and then these invisible messengers pass such instruction on to the remnant.

What an admission! The Governing Body of Jehovah's Witnesses, consisting of several very elderly men who claim to be "the remnant," form all doctrine for Jehovah's Witnesses. How, you may ask? According to a book by a former member of the Governing Body, it wasn't by prayer or study of the Bible (*Crisis of Conscience*, by Raymond Franz). It was supposed to be under "angelic direction," but Raymond Franz left because he felt it was a manmade organization.

However, the Watch Tower Society has frequently made the claim that all they do is by "angelic direction." By their own admission, this happens invisibly. This is odd, because angels appeared many times to God's chosen ones and were actually seen.

Since the "remnant" doesn't actually see these angels, by their own admission, what is going on? One can only assume that they "hear voices" or perhaps receive "truths" by "automatic handwriting," or some such procedure.

If this body of men really are the remnant referred to in the Bible, as Jehovah's Witnesses believe, then they must fulfill Revelation 14:5, which speaks of this special group of the 144,000:

> No lie was found in their mouth; they are blameless.

Not only do we have a history of lying going back over 100 years, but what about these "angels" who direct them?

They do admit that they have things "put in their minds." Consider their admission of this in *Light*, volume 1, 1930, page 120:

> Again God put it in the mind of his people, by his angel, to act and to carry out his purposes.

I can't find a single Bible precedent for angels putting things in the minds of believers. The Holy

Spirit can motivate us, perhaps at times through our minds, but angels? The warning on angels and men preaching a false gospel has direct application to the Watch Tower Society. Galatians 1:8,9 reads:

> Even though we or an angel from heaven should preach to you a gospel contrary to that which we have preached to you, let him be accursed. As we have said before, so I say again now, if any man is preaching to you a gospel contrary to that which you received, let him be accursed

What kind of angels are directing the Society and its "gospel"? They are not preaching the same gospel as the apostles, but a contrary one.

Also disturbing is the claim that angels direct the writing of the *Watchtower* magazine, the prime channel for Jehovah's Witnesses:

> The Lord used the *Watchtower* to announce these truths. Doubtless he used his invisible deputies to have much to do with it (*Light*, Vol. 1, 1930, page 64).

Did God really send His angels to the Watch Tower Organization with these false dates for the end of the world: 1874, 1879, 1914, 1915, 1918, 1925, 1941, 1975? Of course not! If these false dates did not come from God (and they didn't!), can we just excuse them as "honest mistakes"?

No, they cannot be excused, on the basis of Jeremiah 23:16:

Thus says the Lord of hosts, "Do not listen to the words of the prophets who are prophesying to you. They are leading you into futility; they speak a vision of their own imagination, not from the mouth of the Lord.

Again, the truth of prophecies is shown by their fulfillment, as in Jeremiah 28:9:

The prophet who prophesies of peace, when the word of the prophet shall come to pass, then that prophet will be known as one whom the Lord has truly sent.

In biblical times, a prophet whose prophecies failed was taken outside the city gates and stoned to death.

Jehovah's Witnesses have been misled by false prophets again and again down through their history. This is not of God. Pagan practices, however, always produce false predictions. One has only to read the horoscopes to see how many of the predictions of our modern-day stargazers have failed miserably, proving that they were never inspired by God.

Jehovah's Witnesses down through the years have adopted pagan practices such as numerology, stargazing, the zodiac, false predictions, demonic sources, and deliberate mistranslation of the Scriptures in order to bolster up their organization's teachings, but their record stands for itself: They are consistently false.

We join with Jeremiah, a true prophet, who chastised the false prophet Hananiah:

> Listen now, Hananiah, the Lord has not sent you, and you have made this people trust in a lie (Jeremiah 28:15).

Joe was very shaken to learn that while he thought he had been serving God, he had really been deceived by an organization with pagan, occultic roots.

CHAPTER 12

Prophecies of the Watch Tower Society

J oe now turned his attention to the claim of the Jehovah's Witnesses to be God's prophet. They even taught that as one of Jehovah's Witnesses, he was a prophet too. That made him feel responsible for the prophecies of the Watch Tower Bible and Tract Society, of which he was a member. He took out the material Brenda had received and began to read.

Jehovah's Witnesses Claim to Be Prophets

The *Watchtower* of April 1, 1972, page 197, had this statement:

> So, does Jehovah have a prophet to help them, to warn them of dangers and to declare things to come? . . . These questions can be answered in the affirmative. Who is this prophet? . . . This "prophet" was not one man, but was a body of men and women. It was the small group of footstep followers of Jesus Christ, known at that time as International Bible Students. Today they are known as Jehovah's Christian witnesses. . . . Of course it is easy to

say that this group acts as a "prophet" of God. It is another thing to prove it. The only way that this can be done is to review the record. What does it show?

Since the Witnesses claim to be God's prophet, we are free to put them to the Bible test for a prophet, found in Deuteronomy 18:18-20. Verse 22 of this chapter says:

> When a prophet speaks in the name of the Lord [YHWH], if the thing does not come about or come true, that is the thing which the Lord has not spoken.

Verse 20 plainly says, "That prophet shall die." False prophecy cannot be "explained away" and treated lightly. The Watch Tower has invited us to examine their record, and we will! All quotes are from publications of the Watch Tower Bible & Tract Society and are available at headquarters in Brooklyn, New York. Some of these publications may also be found in local Kingdom Hall libraries. Judge this self-proclaimed "prophet" for yourselves!

6000 Years of Human History

6000 years from Adam ended in A.D. 1872 (*Daily Heavenly Manna*, inside cover page).

6000 years of human history ended in 1873 (*The Time Is at Hand*, page 33).

6000 years of human history ended in 1972 (*The Truth Shall Make You Free*, page 152, 1943 edition).

6000 years of human history ended in 1975 (*Awake!* October 8, 1968, page 15).

Armageddon

Armageddon would end in 1914 (*The Time Is at Hand*, page 101, 1911 edition).

Armageddon would end in 1915 (*The Time Is at Hand*, page 101, 1915 edition).

Today, J.W.'s expect Armageddon any minute!

The Return of Christ

Since Christ failed to show up for any of the Watch Tower dates, J.W.'s altered their teaching to make his coming conveniently "invisible."

Christ returned in 1874 (*The Finished Mystery*, pages 295, 386, 1917 edition). The Watch Tower publications taught this 1874 date right up to 1929.

The *Prophecy* book published in 1929 states on page 65:

> The Scriptural proof is that the second presence of the Lord Jesus Christ began in 1874 A.D.

Christ returned in 1914 (*The Truth that Leads to Eternal Life*, page 87).

The Millennium

The Millennium began in 1873 (*Thy Kingdom Come*, page 305).

The Millennium began in 1874 (*Finished Mystery*, page 386).

The Resurrection

The resurrection would occur in 1878 (*Thy Kingdom Come*, page 234).

Abraham, Isaac, Jacob, and the faithful prophets of old would return in 1925 (*Millions Now Living Will Never Die*, page 89).

The Watch Tower Society even published a book telling their followers to add a room onto their houses, and get an undertaker to decorate it. Undertakers, of course, would be looking for employment, since there would be no more deaths in 1926.

When the room was completed, Watch Tower devotees were to call up Jerusalem, where Abraham would have an office, and request that their parents be "awakened" from death. They would soon appear in the new room! (*The Way to Paradise*, pages 228, 229).

Space Travel

Man cannot by airplane or rockets or other means get above the air envelope which is about our earthly globe (*The Truth Shall Make You Free*, page 285, 1943 edition).

The Book of Ruth

The Book of Ruth is "not prophetical" (*Watchtower Reprints* IV, page 3110, Dec. 7, 1902).

The Book of Ruth "is prophetic" (Watch Tower Book, *Preservation*, pages 169, 175, 176).

Sodom and Gomorrah

Sodom and Gomorrah will receive a second opportunity (*Plan of the Ages*, page 110).

Sodom and Gomorrah will receive no second opportunity (*Watchtower*, Feb. 1954, page 85).

Sodom and Gomorrah will receive a second opportunity (*Watchtower*, Mar. 1965, page 139).

This rebounding back and forth as to whether the people of Sodom and Gomorrah will take part in the resurrection has gone on throughout Watch Tower history and continues to this day. Society literature has said "yes" four times and "no" four times over the last 125 years!

The "Higher Powers" of Romans 13:1

"Higher powers" refers to earthly governments (*The Time Is at Hand*, 1889, page 81).

"Higher powers" refers to Jehovah God and Jesus (*The Truth Shall Make You Free*, page 312).

"Higher powers" refers to earthly governments (*Man's Salvation . . . at Hand*, page 326).

The Revelation Name "Abaddon-Apollyon"

Refers to Satan (*Studies in the Scriptures*, Vol. 7).

Refers to Jesus Christ (*Then Is Finished the Mystery of God*, page 232).

Quite a change!

The "Alpha and Omega" of Revelation

Refers to Jehovah God (*Awake!* Aug. 22, 1978, page 28).

Refers to Jesus Christ (*Watchtower*, Oct. 1, 1978, page 15).

Notice the rapid change of "truth" and "interpretation of Scripture" in just two months!

The Faithful and Discreet Slave

Refers to their founder, Charles Taze Russell (*Watchtowers* from 12/1/16 to 3/1/23, page 68).

Refers to the "Remnant of Spiritual Israelites" (the supposed remnant of the 144,000 "heavenly class") (*From Paradise Lost to Paradise Regained*, page 193).

In Conclusion

The official publication of the Jehovah's Witnesses claims:

> ... Jehovah's witnesses today make their declaration of the good news of the kingdom under angelic direction and support.

According to the *Watchtower* of April 1, 1972, page 200, they have proved to be an embarrassment to the angels!

Undaunted, the *Watchtower* of July 1, 1973, page 402, goes on to claim:

> Consider too the fact that Jehovah's organization alone in all the earth is directed by God's holy spirit or active force.

Obviously the Holy Spirit did not prompt these false prophecies!

Not only does the Bible give us a simple test for prophets (which we considered at the beginning, namely that their prophecies will fail), but the Word of God has more to say about prophecies and prophesying.

The Bible reveals three sources for prophecy.

One, it is from God, and inspired by Him. Two, it is from the Devil and inspired by him. Three, prophecies can come out of "the flesh," or out of our "own spirit."

Since the Watch Tower Society of Jehovah's Witnesses has so many failed prophecies, we know they are not prophesying by God's direction, and through His Holy Spirit, or by the angels.

This leaves us with two alternatives for the false prophecies of the Watch Tower Society. They are either from Satan or they are from "the flesh."

The *Watchtower* has chosen the latter, claiming that "we all make mistakes" and "we have new light." Is this an "out" for them? No, for Jehovah's Witnesses should carefully read Ezekiel chapter 13.

This chapter is a judgment of God on prophets who hope for a fulfillment of their words after prophesying falsely. Verse 8 says:

> "Because you have spoken falsehood and seen a lie, therefore behold, I am against you," declares the Lord God.

The Watch Tower Society of Jehovah's Witnesses is a proven false prophet, and the Lord by His own decree is against them. Why would you want to remain in this doomed organization and share in its judgment?

When he was finished examining all the evidence, Joe could only conclude that he had been cruelly deceived by the Watch Tower headquarters. He knew he was not the only one, but Kingdom Halls all over the world were filled with honest-hearted persons like himself who were likewise deceived. He thanked God for the ministries bringing these matters to light, and he thanked God for concerned Christians like Beverly Williams.

He sat down and composed a lengthy letter of disassociation. He wanted to make sure the elders knew exactly why he was leaving. He knew this information would be seen by at least three men in leadership, and he hoped a copy would be sent on to headquarters, where others might see it. He intended to mail a copy to selected ones in the congregation as well. He prayed that God would use his experiences to help others. He knew the elders would be by after a time, so he waited and prepared for their visit.

✦

CHAPTER 13

Leaving the Watch Tower Society

There are several ways out of the Jehovah's Witnesses. Some people just drift away and get lost in the crowd, usually never speaking of their experiences. Some carry tremendous guilt, feeling they could not live up to the requirements. Some leave, but continue to feel they have left "the truth." They carry with them always a vague dread of Armageddon and God's judgment.

Some of these guilty, quiet ones have committed such dreadful sins as refusing to quit smoking, taking or agreeing to a blood transfusion to save a life, or marrying out of the group. If they leave the area without confrontation with the elders, they might get away without a humiliating announcement at the Kingdom Hall of their "wickedness"; they simply move away and never contact the Witnesses again. If Witnesses call at their door in their new location, they politely refuse to talk. They are in hiding.

Others are "disciplined" by the elders for their "sins," and made to "repent" publicly. Some must attend the Kingdom Hall for a full year, knowing that no one will speak to them in or out of the Hall. They suffer greatly, all in the hopes that the elders will see fit to "reinstate" them at the end of their shunning period. This takes a tremendous toll on their physical and spiritual well-being, and many are never the same after this unloving treatment, although they remain Jehovah's Witnesses.

Then there are those who decide to leave the organization for various reasons. They soon find that there is no honorable way out of the Watch Tower Society of Jehovah's Witnesses. They will be shunned, even if they are without "sin."

Any honest-hearted questioning of the Society's doctrines, history, or decisions of the elders results in charges of "apostasy." The person is usually publicly maligned from the platform as his disfellowshiping announcement is read. Innuendos are rampant, especially after he is disfellowshiped for "conduct unbefitting a Christian," one of their favorite announcements that often has nothing to do with one's conduct as such. The "conduct unbefitting a Christian" announcement usually applies equally to smokers, transfusion-takers, adulterers, murderers, and "apostates."

There is only one way to avoid this high-handed and dishonest treatment. That is for the person leaving to take the time to compose a letter of disassociation, giving his or her reasons for leaving. He or she has the option to meet personally with the committee or not at this point. It is necessary to threaten the Society with legal action if they try to make their usual slanderous announcement. This often results in a short announcement being made at the Kingdom Hall that the person in question has disassociated himself. While shocking to the congregation, and the subject of much speculation and gossip, at least the disassociated one has made it plain that he left. He was not thrown out.

Joe chose to disassociate himself. His lengthy disassociation letter shared the truth on Christ, on the history and false prophecies of the organization, and on his newfound relationship with Christ.

Joe assembled all his photocopies of the Society's false prophecies and changing "light" along with his letter of disassociation, and he waited for the elders to show up.

He was not disappointed. They did show up in a very militant frame of mind and attempted to order him around and intimidate him as they had in the past. Imagine their reaction when they were greeted by a strong man who openly invited them to examine his evidence! They refused and left with his disassociation letter firmly in hand.

Joe had closed a chapter in his life. He had learned much about himself. He had placed himself in bondage and then been set free by Christ. He had broken up his marriage and then seen it restored. He had lost a job and along with it his self-respect. Now he would lose another job due to his decision for Christ, but he knew he would make it through on Christ's strength, and by leaning on the abiding love of his wife and family. He was no longer vulnerable and seeking, but he was living his life in a relationship with his Savior, Jesus Christ. He sank back in his chair and smiled at the future.

He had many things to look forward to. Brenda and he had already enjoyed some times of fellowship with new Christian friends whom he had met at Beverly Williams' church. He had prospects of employment. He had begun already to intercede in prayer for the deliverance of Leo Stern and his family from the Jehovah's Witnesses. His daughter Lisa had given her heart to the Lord, and both his family and Brenda's were curious about their new life and faith.

Yes, life with the Lord was not only satisfying but exciting! It was great to be free in Christ.

The Witness at Your Door

The story of the book
*What You Need to Know About
Jehovah's Witnesses*

Attention Pastors and Teachers!

A teacher's manual and student's manual are available so "What You Need to Know About Jehovah's Witnesses" can be taught in your church classes.

For details and ordering information, please write:

MacGregor Ministries
Box 591
Point Roberts, WA 98281
USA

In Canada and Overseas
Box 73
Balfour, B.C. V0G 1C0
Canada

☐ Yes, please send me your free catalog and price list for Christian videos.

☐ Yes, please send me details on your teacher and student manuals.

Name _____

Address _____

State _____ Code _____

Conversations
with the Cults Series

Each book in this intriguing series examines a popular cult, providing critical information about what members of the sect usually say when questioned about their religion. In the unique format of a docudrama, the authors use easy-to-understand language to unravel the double meanings of the cults' beliefs and explain the contradictions of their seemingly "Christian" answers. *The author of each book is a recognized expert who has come out of the cult and knows it from the inside out.*

What You Need to Know
About Jehovah's Witnesses
— Lorri MacGregor —

One day in his devoted work for the Watch Tower Society, Joe Simpson finds himself on the doorstep of a concerned Christian who has learned how to talk to Jehovah's Witnesses. In the resulting conversations, the key elements of Jehovah's Witnesses doctrine are clearly refuted with Christian love and Scripture.

What You Need to Know
About Masons
— Ed Decker —

When Jeff Moore, a young Baptist minister, resigns from the Lodge, his family and his church relationships are thrown into chaos. The hidden dangers of Free-masonry are fully communicated and its secret initiation ceremonies exposed in this creative approach to one of the least-recognized cults.

What You Need to Know
About Mormons
— Ed Decker —

The differences between Mormonism and Christianity are clearly presented through a series of conversations between neighbors, which sheds light on the tenets of Mormonism and the countering truths of the Bible.

Other Good
Harvest House Reading

WITNESSES OF JEHOVAH
A Shocking Exposé of What Jehovah's Witnesses Really Believe
by *Leonard* and *Marjorie Chretien*

Two ex-Jehovah's Witnesses candidly reveal the hidden facts about the Watchtower Society in order to expose this harmful pseudo-Christian organization for what it is.

COPING WITH THE CULTS
by *Lorri MacGregor*

Hands on, down-to-earth explanations and an evangelistic focus make *Coping with the Cults* the winning choice in a popular guide to the cults. The author's extensive personal ministry to cult groups for the past 15 years lets her target the main points quickly and thoroughly in simple, nontechnical language. Easy-to-remember questions help readers determine whether an unfamiliar group is a cult.

CULT WATCH
by *John Ankerberg* and *John Weldon*

Cult Watch provides historical background and the vital facts on the major beliefs of modern religious movements and looks closely at the reasons people become entrapped in them. Drawing from years of research and interaction with representatives of each movement, the authors offer penetrating analysis of how each religious system clearly contrasts with the essential doctrines of biblical Christianity.

ANSWERS TO THE CULTIST AT YOUR DOOR
by *Robert* and *Gretchen Passantino*

This book is for anyone who wants a basic understanding of the cults without undue research! Concise reviews and answers to the beliefs of Jehovah's Witnesses, Hare Krishnas, The Way International, Mormons, and Moonies. Highly recommended by Walter Martin.

Dear Reader:

We would appreciate hearing from you regarding this Harvest House nonfiction book. It will enable us to continue to give you the best in Christian publishing.

1. What most influenced you to purchase *What You Need to Know About Jehovah's Witnesses?*
   - ☐ Author
   - ☐ Subject matter
   - ☐ Backcover copy
   - ☐ Recommendations
   - ☐ Cover/Title
   - ☐ _____

2. Where did you purchase this book?
   - ☐ Christian bookstore
   - ☐ General bookstore
   - ☐ Department store
   - ☐ Grocery store
   - ☐ Other

3. Your overall rating of this book:
   ☐ Excellent   ☐ Very good   ☐ Good   ☐ Fair   ☐ Poor

4. How likely would you be to purchase other books by this author?
   - ☐ Very likely
   - ☐ Somewhat likely
   - ☐ Not very likely
   - ☐ Not at all

5. What types of books most interest you? (check all that apply)
   - ☐ Women's Books
   - ☐ Marriage Books
   - ☐ Current Issues
   - ☐ Self Help/Psychology
   - ☐ Bible Studies
   - ☐ Fiction
   - ☐ Biographies
   - ☐ Children's Books
   - ☐ Youth Books
   - ☐ Other _____

6. Please check the box next to your age group.
   - ☐ Under 18
   - ☐ 18-24
   - ☐ 25-34
   - ☐ 35-44
   - ☐ 45-54
   - ☐ 55 and over

Mail to: Editorial Director
Harvest House Publishers
1075 Arrowsmith
Eugene, OR 97402

Name _____

Address _____

City _____ State _____ Zip _____

**Thank you for helping us to help you
in future publications!**